How To Grow Potatoes

Jason Johns

Visit me at www.GardeningWithJason.com for gardening tips and advice or follow me at www.YouTube.com/OwningAnAllotment for my video diary and tips. Join me on Facebook at www.Facebook.com/OwningAnAllotment.

Follow me on Instagram and Twitter as @allotmentowner for regular updates, tips and to ask your gardening questions.

If you have enjoyed this book, please leave a review. I read each review personally and the feedback helps me to continually improve my books and provide you with more helpful books to read.

Once you have read this book, you will be offered a chance to download one of my books for free. Please turn to the back of this book now to find out how to get your free book.

TABLE OF CONTENTS

INTRODUCTION

Potatoes are a staple food in Western cultures, whether they are served as fries, roasted, baked or included in any number of dishes. They are grown in huge quantities across the world by farmers and are one of the most popular and easiest vegetable crops to grow at home, second only to tomatoes. They can be grown in the ground or in containers and are a relatively low maintenance crop.

When you buy potatoes from the supermarket you are limited to a few "popular" varieties. The most common variety found tends to be Maris Piper as a large potato whereas new potatoes tend to be Charlotte or Jersey potatoes. High end potatoes tend to be Red Rooster or a similar purple variety. Most varieties in supermarket, like other vegetables, are not necessarily chosen because of their flavor, but are chosen on their uniform appearance, how well they store and their ability to be transported. At the end of the day, this is what concerns supermarkets as potatoes can be shipped all over the world and the crop needs to last until it is in the consumer's kitchen.

The advantage of growing your own potatoes at home is that you can grow some of the more interesting and more delicious varieties of potatoes that you will never find in a supermarket. Although I enjoy growing Maris Piper potatoes I get a special delight out of growing the weirdly shaped Pink Fur Apple or a Nicola or a Salad Blue. Serving your dinner guests purple potatoes is always a delight (try roasting them with golden beetroot for a very colorful meal).

Growing potatoes is incredibly simple to do and they can be grown in the ground, in special containers or even in something as simple as a bucket! Kids love growing potatoes and get very excited when it comes to harvest time.

You can grow as many or as few potatoes as you like because potatoes, unlike many other vegetables, will store for some months in the correct conditions. Many people I know grow vast amounts of potatoes and then store them for use well into winter.

This book will teach you everything you need to know about successfully growing your own potatoes and growing interesting varieties that are much nicer than those you find in the stores. Towards the end of the book you will find an in-depth guide to some of the different varieties and it is definitely worth trying some of these.

You'll find out everything about growing potatoes from selecting seed potatoes, the differences between the earlies, maincrop and late plus how to get your potatoes started so they germinate and grow well.

As you read this book you will also learn all about how to plant your potatoes whether you plant them in the ground, in containers or in raised beds. We'll discuss the pros and cons of the different growing methods plus how to get the best results from each one.

Harvesting and storing your potatoes will also be covered so that you know the best way to store your potatoes for them to last a good few months. Of course, for many of us, potatoes never last that long because they all get eaten!

Potatoes do suffer from some problems with pests and diseases which you will learn about as you read through this book. You will discover some of the potential problems, how to minimize the risk of contracting them, plus what to do if your potatoes do get infested or infected.

Finally, I will share with you some of my favorite potato recipes and, don't worry, it isn't going to be just fries! I will share with you the absolute best (and healthiest) way to cook potatoes to really make them delicious.

Growing potatoes is really good fun and something that can be done with a minimal investment of time. You don't need to spend lots of money on equipment and can grow potatoes that can be harvested for many months of the year.

Enjoy learning all about growing potatoes and how to get a fantastic crop from them. There is a lot to learn but as you get down to it you will be surprised by just how easy and how much fun this is!

A BRIEF HISTORY OF POTATOES

Potatoes are the fourth largest cultivated food crop in the world after rice, wheat and maize, as well as being one of the most popular home grown crops. Potatoes originated in South America where the Incas in Peru began to cultivate them in the Andes somewhere between 8,000BC and 5,000BC. There are over 4000 varieties of native potatoes grown in this region, coming in every shape, size and color from blue to pink to yellow to red and purple.

In 1536, after the Spanish conquered Peru, they discovered the joys of the potato and returned triumphantly to Europe bearing this now staple crop. Before the end of the century potatoes were being cultivated in northern Spain and in 1589 Sir Walter Raleigh planted 40,000 acres of potatoes near Cork in Ireland. Over the next forty years the potato spread throughout Europe, becoming more and more popular.

Potatoes were discovered to be very easy to grow, much easier than oats and wheat which were the staple crop up until then. Potatoes were discovered to contain a high level of vitamins, essential to humans and that a single acre of land would provide enough potatoes for ten people.

Europe came to rely heavily on the potato for food. So much so, that when potato blight struck in the 1840's it wiped out the food source for millions of people. In Ireland, where the working class literally lived on potatoes, the blight caused a massive famine and many families died or left the country in order to survive. This famine killed over a million people and a similar number left Ireland for the United States and Canada.

In 1621 potatoes arrived in North America when Nathaniel Butler, the Governor of Bermuda, sent two large chests of potatoes to Governor Francis Wyatt of Jamestown, Virginia. In around 1719 potato crops were established in New Hampshire, near Londonderry and the vegetable then spread with the settlers across the rest of the country.

Today, the largest producer of potatoes in the United States is Idaho, though it wasn't until 1836 that the potato was introduced by missionaries into this state. The industry didn't take off until the Russet Burbank variety was developed in 1872. It is not surprising to know that Idaho is known as 'the potato state' as it produces around a third of all the potatoes consumed in the United States. Over 300,000 acres are set aside in this state for potato growing and over 100 million hundredweight are produced each year.

In France, potatoes became popular in the 18th century under the reign of King Louis XIV and French fries were introduced into the USA during the presidency of Thomas Jefferson who served them in the White House. The 19th century saw a lot of experimentation with potatoes and many of the dishes we take for granted today such as potato chips and soufflés were created in this time.

Potatoes have proven to be a reliable staple crop and there are close to 5,000 different varieties of potato across the world. During the Klondike gold rush in Alaska (1897-1898) potatoes were as valuable as gold because they were high in vitamin C, which was otherwise hard to get from the normal diet at the time. In 1995 potatoes had the honor of becoming the first vegetable to be grown in space.

Today, the potato is still a popular crop and can be found in a wide variety of meals and products. Whether you like your potatoes roasted, boiled, baked, mashed, chipped or fried, it is a great crop to grow at home and one you will enjoy learning about as you read this book.

SELECTING SEED POTATOES

To grow potatoes, you need to buy seed potatoes. Seed potatoes are not actually seeds but are smaller potatoes which form sprouts that then grow into the actual plant. Most people buy seed potatoes from a nursery or store but the more unusual varieties are harder to find unless you look online. Online retailers will sell a much wider variety of seed potatoes.

While you can sometimes grow potato plants from store bought potatoes, it is not recommended. You do not know if these are disease free and some will not grow into usable potatoes for some reason. Some store bought potatoes are sprayed with a chemical that prevents them from producing sprouts and the potato actually rots before the leaves form. Although a store bought potato may look okay on the outside, you don't know whether is harboring a disease which will wipe out your crop. Saying that though, many people successfully grow from store bought potatoes.

You can save potatoes from the previous year's harvest but these can harbor disease and need storing carefully so they survive until planting time.

Personally, I buy seed potatoes because I know I am getting a variety I want and I know they are disease free. I tend to grow first earlies purely to avoid blight which is common in my area and I tend to grow some new (small) potatoes and some larger potatoes. You'll find details later on in this book about the many varieties available to you. I like to buy the varieties I want rather than grow the two or three found in most supermarkets.

Depending on where you are, there are often swap meets for seeds and potatoes where you can take your seed potatoes and swap them with other people or you can buy unusual, heritage potato varieties. If any are run in your area, then they are well worth a visit as you can find some very unusual local varieties. Usually, I end up swapping some of my seed potatoes with people on my allotment site for some of theirs. This way we all get a nice variety of potatoes and almost everyone I know ends up with left over seed potatoes they haven't got the space to plant.

As your potato plants mature you may notice green round pods forming where the flowers were. These often cause confusion with some people wondering if they are tomatoes or edible. Please do not touch these at all as they are poisonous. They are potato seeds but no-one grows potatoes from these seeds.

One advantage of potatoes is that they don't cross pollinate so if you are planting a Yukon Gold seed potato then you know you are going to end up with a crop of Yukon Gold potatoes! Unfortunately, we can't say the same for squashes which can cross pollinate and produce inedible varieties.

When choosing your seed potatoes, you are looking for most of them to be around the size of a chicken egg. If some are larger then don't worry as you can still use them but ideally you want most to be about this size. Look for ones that are showing signs of budding so you know they are viable and will grow when you plant them. Some seed potatoes simply do not form sprouts and therefore do not grow. Note that maincrop seed potatoes tend to be larger purely because the resulting potatoes are larger.

Typically, most potato varieties will need between 70 and 90 days from planting until they are mature. First earlies mature the quickest and maincrop take longer for the potatoes to grow to full size. Smaller types of potatoes do not tend to store as well as the larger ones.

How Many Seed Potatoes to Buy?

Seed potatoes are usually sold by weight rather than quantity in stores. Attending a swap meet does mean you can pick a quantity (which is often then weighed). How many you get in a net (which is what they are contained in) will depend on the type of potato – some varieties of potatoes are larger seed than others.

If you are growing in the ground, first early potatoes need to be planted 12"/30cm apart with 16-20"/40-50cm between rows. Second earlies and maincrop varieties grow larger so need more space; 15"/38cm between plants and 30"/75cm between rows. If you are growing in bags, each potato bag can have 3 to 5 potatoes depending on variety and the size of the bag.

It is a bit hit and miss how many potatoes you end up with due to a variety of factors including how much rain there is, how hot it is and so on. I'd recommend looking at some potato nets in the stores to give you a rough idea of how many potatoes you get to the pound or kilogram. Most years I buy too many potatoes and end up planting them in buckets and bags as well as giving them to fellow allotment holders.

Difference Between 1st Early, 2nd Early, Maincrop and Late Potatoes

This is where some people get a little bit confused because the descriptions aren't particularly helpful, so let me just explain the difference between them so you know exactly what you are going to grow.

Ultimately, it is the time it takes for the potatoes to mature that determines which category they fall into, though there are other subtle differences too.

First early potatoes are usually planted towards the end of March. They are planted at a depth of 4"/10cm and 12"/30cm is left between plants in a row. The distance between rows is recommended to be 24-28"/60-70cm. First earlies are usually ready from the beginning to the middle of June and are often favored because they are ready before blight and other pests really take hold. Some of my favorite early varieties include Nicola, Vivaldi, Charlotte and Maris Peer potatoes, all well worth trying in my opinion.

Second earlies are planted early to mid-April, also at a depth of 4"/10cm with 12-16"/30-40cm between seed potatoes and 28-30"/70-75cm) left between rows. Second earlies take between 15 and 17 weeks to mature meaning they are ready anywhere from the middle of June to the start of August, depending on when they were planted.

Maincrop potatoes are planted from mid to late April with 16-18"/40-45cm between seed potatoes and 28-30"/70-75cm between rows. Maincrop potatoes take longer to mature, somewhere between 18 and 20 weeks, depending on the variety, and are lifted any time from July through to October. Maincrop are very popular and are the best potatoes to grow if you are planning on storing them.

Late potatoes are a relatively new variety and are not that common. These are typically planted in June or July and are ready to lift at Christmas. Anyone who likes to grow their own Christmas dinner is likely to plant one of these. If you live in an area with a lot of rainfall between September and December, then you will want to grow in containers rather than the soil to protect your crop from rot. If the ground freezes solid where you live, then these will need to be dug up before the ground is too hard to dig.

Which type of potato you grow will depend on your preferences and what you are planning on doing with them. Most people will grow a combination of all four varieties simply so they have fresh potatoes throughout the year. Anyone who lives in an area susceptible to blight is better off planting first earlies as they are usually harvested before blight strikes.

CHITTING SEED POTATOES

Before you plant your potatoes, you should always chit them, which encourages them to sprout and grow before you put them in the ground. If the weather is warm enough and the ground is warm, then they will sprout in the soil. However, earlier in the season when the soil is cool, chitting your potatoes will give them a head start. Often this can mean an earlier harvest and sometimes even time for a second crop! Because potatoes are quite a long season vegetable, chitting indoors gives them more time to grow and mature. Note that late season potatoes do not require chitting because they are cold stored and start to grow as soon as they are removed from storage.

To chit potatoes you first need to take your seed potato and determine which side has the most eyes (sprouts). Ideally, you are looking for at least four and on one end which is designated the top. Remove any other eyes so that the sprouts are all growing in one direction. You may need to turn the potato a few times to determine which side is best being the 'top'. Sometimes, the seed potatoes need to be planted on their side in order for the eyes to face upward.

Put the potatoes in a bright, dry (but not sunny) place in a shallow box or egg carton. This will encourage strong green shots, rather than the weak white ones found on eating potatoes that have been left in the dark. Most people leave them on a window sill but you can leave them outside, providing they will not be caught in a frost. Remember to protect your seed potatoes from mice as they will chew and damage them.

Sometimes you will see a spot on the plant that looks like it is forming roots and if so, this needs to go face down as it will form roots in the ground. This is usually the point where the potato was connected to the mother plant.

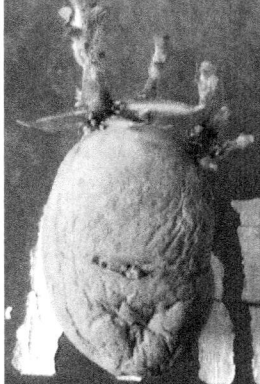

Not everyone chits their potatoes, but I find that chitting them for 3 to 4 weeks gives them a bit of a head start so I can get them in the ground sooner. It means they have started growing and will "take" much quicker when you put them in the soil. Although you can just put seed potatoes straight in the soil they will generally take longer to sprout and grow, particularly if the soil is cold.

When they have grown sprouts, usually in three or four weeks, then you are ready to put them in the ground.

Cutting Seed Potatoes

Some seed potatoes are larger than others, and it does seem a waste to plant one giant potato. One of my favorite tricks is to cut a larger seed potato into two or three pieces. You need to make sure that each piece has eyes on it that will develop into shoots, but this will give you more seed potatoes for your money.

Most seed potatoes are about the size of chicken eggs, but occasionally there are bigger ones and they will grow just fine if you carefully cut them using this method. Chit them as normal and then cut them a day or two before you plan to put them in the ground.

After you have cut the potato leave it somewhere cool and dry for 24 to 48 hours with the cut edge facing upwards to allow it to dry and form a protective membrane. Once this has formed then you can plant it. Planting a cut seed potato without allowing it to dry can cause it to rot.

Protecting Potatoes From Frost

Seed potatoes are susceptible to frost damage as the new growth is particularly tender. You need to ensure they are in an area where they are protected from frosts. Most people will chit them on a window sill or in a shed where they will not be damaged by frosts but you can chit them outside. You just have to be careful if you do and bring them in if there is a risk of frost.

As potatoes are chitted four to six weeks before planting they are often at risk of frost damage so look after them. Frost will kill the tender shoots and delay your potato crop or even completely kill the seed potato.

When you plant your potatoes out you also need to watch out for new growth coming up out of the ground. This is also tender and can be damaged by frost. If there is a risk of frost earth up over the new growth to protect it and it will continue growing and push through the earth.

In the case of a particularly late frost when the potatoes can't be earthed up or if you do not have time to earth them up, cover the potatoes with horticultural fleece to protect them from the frost. As frost warnings can often by last minute, this happens more than you may think. If the foliage does get caught in a frost, it will turn black and die. In some cases, the potatoes can survive this, but if it is too late in the season, it will kill the plants and they will not produce potatoes.

Planting Potatoes

 A lot of people will plant their potatoes in the ground rather than in containers, which we will discuss in the next chapter. This is probably the most popular way of planting potatoes and the one we are all most familiar with. If you want you can grow potatoes in straw bales which is detailed in my book Straw Bale Gardening – No Dig, No Bending Productive Vegetable Gardens available online and in all good bookstores.

Potatoes are pretty tolerant plants and like a soil that is rich in compost but they will also do well in a poor soil, particularly if you add some fertilizer and feed regularly.

A heavy clay soil is problematical for potatoes simply because it gets waterlogged which then causes the tubers to either rot or not form properly. A wet soil also attracts pests like slugs and your potatoes get nibbled on. However, amending the soil with gypsum or plenty of manure the autumn before planting can help break up the soil so it is better for your potatoes. In fact, potatoes are quite good themselves at helping to break up soil! Note that if you are adding manure to the soil, make sure it is well-rotted before you plant your potatoes otherwise it increases the incidence of potato scab.

The potato plants themselves are usually left alone by pests as both the stems and leaves are toxic. However, some smarter animals will dig up the tubers and eat them.

Crop Rotation and Potatoes

Crop rotation should be used when planting potatoes and they should be on a three or four-year rotation plan, i.e. don't plant them in the same place two years in a row. Typically, you will wait three or four years before planting them in the same spot again. This will mean that any potatoes that appear from ones left in the ground (and this will happen) should be removed as soon as they sprout.

This is very important because potatoes are susceptible to diseases and the pathogens can live in the soil. By rotating your crops, you stop the build-up of these pathogens and reduce your reliance on chemical treatments.

Although you can buy disease (usually blight) resistant potatoes, you need to be aware these are resistant not immune … there is a difference. Usually it means they still get blight if your area is prone to it, just a bit later on in the season, hopefully after they have been harvested.

Growing Potatoes in Raised Beds

It is possible to grow potatoes in raised beds but I will be honest with you it is a bit of a waste of your raised beds. Unless you struggle to bend and dig then raised beds are not the best place for potatoes.

A raised bed is what we call an expensive resource in a vegetable garden. It has cost money to build and fill with soil and when filled with potatoes they are using a lot of these resource as you can't plant anything else in it until they are finished. Raised beds are often quite small, meaning you cannot get a lot of potato plants in them, so you will need a lot of raised beds for a decent crop of potatoes.

You will also find, and this is my pet hate, potatoes springing up in your raised bed the following year and sometimes for years after. No matter how carefully you dig through the bed you are more than likely going to leave something that will turn into a potato plant. On my allotment I've just uncovered an area that has been under five feet of weeds for about four years (I inherited the weeds) and found potato plants growing!

Rather than use your valuable raised bed for potatoes you are better to either grow in the ground or to grow in containers.

Preparing the Ground

The best position for potatoes is an open one with full sun and a well fertilized, well-drained soil. Potatoes actually prefer a slightly acidic soil, but they will tolerate most soil types. If your soil is particularly alkaline then you can apply some sulfur to the top of the potato ridge once you have planted them. This will help to give a good yield as well as protect against problems such as common scab and other skin blemishes, which are more prevalent in alkaline soils.

You need to start preparing the soil well in advance, usually around November or December time so that it has chance to settle properly. Remove the weeds, dig the site over well, ideally to a two spade depth and pick out any large stones. You will want to dig in some well-rotted organic matter such as horse manure and also a high potash fertilizer to make sure the soil is at its best for your potatoes.

Then you can cover the soil with a tarp or keep an eye on it, removing weeds as they appear. Some people like to give the soil a last dig a week or two before planting to fully aerate it though most people do not think this is necessary.

Planting Potatoes in the Ground

This is where planting potatoes gets a little bit controversial and arguments start so I am going to lay out the different options for you and you can choose which one works for you. I will tell you my favorite method and why then leave it up to you to decide which you prefer. It comes down to time, ability and the amount of effort you want to exert in growing potatoes.

Remember that spacing is very important when planting your potatoes as if they are too close together then your potatoes will be small whereas if the spacing is bigger, you can expect larger potatoes. Most people will leave about 2½ feet between rows of potatoes so there is plenty of room for them to grow.

Trenches vs Mounds

The traditional way of growing potatoes is in trenches, but I will warn you it is hard work digging out the trenches, particularly if you are planting a lot of potatoes. Expect back ache and for it to take a good few hours to do.

A lot of people plant using the trench method but not everyone does. You may find after digging out a few trenches you decide there is a better way to do it or you may prefer to stick to tradition.

The process for trench planting is simple:

1. Dig a trench about a foot deep and a spades width wide, mounding up the soil on either side of the trench
2. Loosen up the soil in the bottom of the trench
3. Put your potatoes in the bottom of the trench with the eyes facing upwards, spaced appropriately
4. Cover the potatoes with about three inches of soil from either side of the trench, leaving the rest of the soil on the sides and firm the soil gently around the potato

Hilling or Earthing Up Your Potatoes

Whether you plant in the ground or in containers you will need to earth up (or hill) your potatoes. This involves scraping the soil left from digging the trench over where the potato plant is growing, then firming it up.

This is important because it supports the plant as it is growing but it is also protects the potatoes from the light. If potatoes are exposed to light, then they turn green and they can make you unwell. Earthing up your potatoes prevents them from going green because light does not get to the tubers. It can also protect tender shoots from frost.

Keep doing this as the plant grows until it starts to flower and then just keep an eye on the plant and earth up more if you see any potatoes becoming exposed. You will usually end up with the potatoes growing in a little hill with a trench on either side, the reverse to how they started.

Growing in Mounds

Growing potatoes in mounds is very similar to the trench method except you don't dig long trenches, just separate holes and then mound up the soil as the plant grows.

People will argue that this is less work but it isn't as popular as the traditional trench method.

George's Method

I've named this after a wonderful 80-year-old allotment owner who shared this with me after watching me struggling digging trenches. This is my favorite way of planting potatoes in the ground and involves a lot less work! I will admit, I had wondered how an 80-year-old man with two artificial hips had managed to plant a dozen long rows of potatoes and now I know!

The process is very simple, you mark out a row and remember the spacing of your potatoes between your rows. Then at every point where a potato should go you push your spade into the ground as far as it will go.

Then wiggle it to either side to make a gap, pulling the spade to one side so you can see the bottom of the hole. Drop your seed potato into this hole with the eyes facing upwards and then remove your spade. Firm up the soil with your boot and move on to the next one.

I love this method because I suffer with back pain and it reduces bending and digging. It is much easier than spending hours and hours digging trenches. The potatoes still grow and are perfectly fine when they come out. The next picture shows you one of my potato beds planted in this way.

Volunteer Potatoes

Anyone who grows potatoes in the ground will quickly learn about volunteer potatoes, also known as donor potatoes.

Potatoes grow from any little potato left in the ground, and it can be very difficult to get them all out of the ground when digging them up. This is one reason some people prefer to grow their potatoes in containers. Any little potato or even part of a potato (where it has been damaged in lifting) can grow into a new plant the following year.

When you practice crop rotation, this means that you end up with potatoes growing in the midst of the current crop. While these can be seen as free potatoes, they are also somewhat annoying as they will disturb and even overcrowd what you are growing at the moment. Worse still, these potatoes could be harboring diseases. In my experience, volunteer potatoes succumb to blight much sooner than freshly planted potatoes.

Unless the bed is fallow, dig up and remove any volunteer potatoes as soon as they poke their heads above the soil. This prevents disturbance of what you are growing currently and stops these old potatoes from spreading disease and providing a haven for pests. They are pretty easy to dig up when they are small, try your best to remove any potatoes attached to the stalk and then dispose of the stalk. Do not compost it as this can aid the spread of disease and pests.

Spacing Potatoes

Planting your potatoes depends on the weather and where in the world you are, but I've put together a table which summarises when to plant potatoes, the spacing and the harvest time. Use your best judgement on when to plant them considering that if the soil is too wet, then the potatoes can rot in the ground.

That will give you a good idea of when to plant your potatoes and how to space them which should make it easier for you to know exactly when to plant your potatoes. The time to harvest will depend on the weather and the amount of rain, but we will talk more about this later in the book. Remember to check your last and first frost dates where you live because these dates will move depending on where you are located.

When growing in raised beds with a high quality soil, the spacing can be a little closer, but proper spacing is required to allow air to circulate around the plants. This can reduce the risk of blight and other fungal infections.

Type	When to plant	Spacing within a row	Distance between rows	Time to harvest
First Earlies	From start of March	12" / 30cm	24" / 60cm	10 weeks from planting
Second Earlies	From mid-March	15" / 37cm	30" / 75cm	13 weeks from planting
Early Main	From late March	18" / 45cm	30" / 75cm	15 weeks from planting
Maincrop	From late March	18" / 45cm	30" / 75cm	20 weeks from planting
Second crop	Early August	12" / 30cm	24" / 60cm	11 weeks from planting

Growing Potatoes With Children

Growing potatoes with children is really good fun and while they are not keen on the maintenance part of growing, they love the harvesting and eating parts. Potatoes are an excellent, low maintenance crop that is ideal to grow with your children or a group of children such as a class at school. They are particularly suitable for schools as if you plant first early potatoes, they will be ready to harvest before the school summer holidays. Most other vegetables ripen when no-one is in the school, but potatoes can be ready in June or early July when planted early.

When growing potatoes with children, they are best grown in potato bags or containers. If you are growing as part of a class or other group of children, it can be made into fun by giving each child a bucket full of compost with their name on. Each child then looks after their potato plant and harvests it before school finishes for the summer. In a bucket you can usually only get one seed potato, but if you are growing first earlies, it is possible to squeeze two seed potatoes in to give the kids a larger crop. Alternatively, split the children into groups and each group gets a potato bag and 4-6 seed potatoes to plant. At home, use whatever you have to hand, even compost bags will do, but grow them in containers rather in the ground.

Growing potatoes is great as it can be used to teach the children about where food comes from and how it is grown. It can be combined with teaching about a plants lifecycle and biology too, making it quite an educational process.

You may have to help the children with watering the potato plants, but it can be a fun activity for them to participate in so they understand the work that goes into caring for plants. As the plants are in containers, there will be no need to weed, which kids generally do not like to do. If the potatoes flower, remove the flowers as soon as they appear so they do not turn into the poisonous seed balls.

Harvest time is when the real fun comes as kids absolutely love harvesting potatoes. Move the bags or buckets to a piece of open soil (such as a flower bed) where it doesn't matter where the soil goes. Avoid doing this on lawn or paved areas as it will make a mess. If you don't have any open soil, then spread a large tarpaulin on the ground to contain the soil.

Tip the container out onto the ground and then let the children dig through the soil with their hands to find the potatoes. When you do this with young children, they get really excited at finding each potato. Then you can either cook with the potatoes with the children or, if it is a school class, send the children home with some potatoes each.

I've grown potatoes a couple of times with groups of school children and they absolutely love the whole process. It is good fun for them and a very good learning experience. They find out a lot about the lifecycle of plants and enjoy the harvesting part more than anything else. Give it a try with your own children or, if you are involved with any groups of children, do it with them. Remember to pick a good first early potato, a decent compost and ensure your containers have drainage holes and you will grow a good crop of potatoes.

Growing Potatoes In Containers

Potatoes are really easy to grow in containers and I will admit I prefer to grow in containers. It means no digging, no preparing the soil and they are really easy to harvest; the kids love tipping over the containers and sifting through the soil for potatoes. It also means I don't spear my potatoes with my fork as I am digging them up or that I leave potatoes in the ground which pop up in the middle of another crop the following year.

You can use any type of container for potatoes, though make sure it has suitable drainage as potatoes do not like being waterlogged and the tubers will rot. Specialist potato bags are available and these are excellent for growing potatoes in.

The number of seed potatoes that will go into a container will depend on the size of the container. The bigger the container, the more potatoes it can support. A bucket is only really big enough for a single potato, but a potato bag or compost bag can support three to five seed potatoes, depending on how big the bag is.

I use potato bags as they are sturdy and usually have handles, meaning I can move them around the plot as I need to. Usually my potatoes are fairly mobile during the growing season because I shift them around depending on what I am planting where and what they will cast shade on. Potato bags are relatively cheap and will last several growing seasons. I usually buy them towards the end of summer when they are reduced in the stores and are even cheaper!

For this size potato bag (shown in the picture above) I plant 3 to 5 potatoes, depending on whether they are late or first early potatoes. First earlies are smaller, so more potatoes can fit in a bag.

The soil used in containers is important. A mixture of a good quality, peat free compost and some top soil is ideal, though use whatever you have to hand or can get hold of. Just remember that the soil should not become waterlogged as it will rot the tubers. Depending on the type of compost and how much it holds water you can add some horticultural sand to the container to help with drainage.

The process for planting seed potatoes in containers is very easy:
1. Fill the bag about half full with the soil mix and firm down
2. Push the potatoes into the soil with the eyes facing upwards until they are a couple of inches under the soil
3. Water well and walk away

You can see in the above picture that the potatoes are positioned in the bag and are ready to be pushed into the soil.

As the potatoes sprout, earth them up by adding more of the soil mix until the bag is just over three quarters full with soil. Then stop earthing them up and only add more soil if the tubers are exposed to the light to prevent them from going green. Usually by this time, the foliage has grown to such an extent that it is shading the tubers, but check anyway as you do not want them to turn green.

Potatoes in containers need watering regularly, even when it has rained as the leaves are pretty good at directing rain away from the soil. It will grow into a veritable jungle so keep an eye on them.

If the weather is particularly wet, then lift the containers up off the ground using bricks or pallets. If the containers are left on the ground they can end up waterlogged as the soil will suck water up through the drainage holes. Keeping the bags off the ground makes such they can drain well and the soil does not end up too wet.

It is important that there is space between your containers so air can flow around the leaves. This helps to prevent blight and fungal infections in the leaves. Do not crowd the containers together and leave plenty of space between them.

Ensure that your container has suitable drainage. Potato bags will have holes in the bottom but if you are using buckets or compost bags then you will need to punch holes in the bottom of them to stop the containers become waterlogged. Remember potatoes are susceptible to rotting in soggy soils so you need to make sure water doesn't build up in it.

Harvesting your potatoes is really simple, just pour the bag out onto the ground (or a tarp) and then root out all the potatoes. The used compost can be put on your compost pile or dug into the ground so it doesn't go to waste.

Containers are a great way to grow potatoes and involve a lot less work, particularly if you are just growing a few plants. Kids love it because they can get involved in the harvesting and they are easy to look after. This is my preferred method of growing potatoes simply because it is quick and easy, though be prepared to use a lot of compost to fill the bags!

PROS & CONS OF GREENHOUSE PLANTING

Potatoes can be grown in a greenhouse but whether you do or not will depend on your personal preference. For many of us, greenhouse space is a premium so tender crops such as tomatoes and chillies are grown under glass. However, at the end of the season, this space becomes free and could realistically be used for potatoes in containers before winter.

If you live in an area prone to a lot of rain, with a short growing season or you want to grow potatoes out of season, then growing in a greenhouse is a good idea. If you live in an area where potatoes will happily grow outside, then don't use it. If your growing season is short, look at short season potatoes or first earlies that mature rapidly rather than growing slower growing, maincrop potatoes.

A greenhouse has a limited amount of space which most gardeners consider to be valuable, i.e. it costs money to buy a greenhouse and you need to make the most of the space. Therefore, as potatoes take up a lot of room they should be grown outside rather than in a greenhouse. This valuable space can then be used for plants that will not grow outside in your area instead such as tomatoes, cucumbers, chillies and so on.

If you do grow your potatoes in a greenhouse, then avoid planting them direct in the soil. They will be difficult to dig up without disturbing your greenhouse or other plants and you will end up with potatoes appearing in your greenhouse for years afterwards. Greenhouse potatoes should always be grown in containers so you can manage them and ensure they don't "escape". Ideally, you want larger containers such as potato bags rather than smaller, single potato containers.

Potatoes need more care in a greenhouse because they will dry out much quicker. Therefore, they need watering much more often, sometimes twice a day during the hottest times of the year.

Air circulation is even more important because the damp, humid environment of a greenhouse can be a haven for fungal problems and blight. Make sure there is plenty of space between the plants so that the air can circulate and keep the leaves dry. Keep the potatoes away from other plants, such as tomatoes, as everything needs sufficient space for the air to circulate to prevent problems.

A lot of people grow tomatoes in greenhouses because they have a long growing season. Tomatoes and potatoes belong to the same family and should not be planted near each other. This means that unless you have a very big greenhouse you should avoid growing potatoes in there if you are already growing tomatoes. The reason behind this is that both plants are susceptible to blight and the blight can transfer between the two, i.e. your tomatoes can infect your potatoes and vice versa. However, if your tomatoes have finished growing in the greenhouse and did not suffer from blight, you can grow potatoes in your greenhouse.

Potatoes will grow well in a greenhouse if you give them plenty of care and attention as they will dry out very quickly because they are in containers. You can shorten the growing period a little by growing them in here though in all but the coldest and wettest areas you are wasting valuable space that could be used to grow plants that are harder to grow outdoors.

I would recommend avoiding growing potatoes in a greenhouse if you can and grow them outside. If your area is chilly then grow them in containers against a sunny wall. The wall will shelter them from the coldest weather and reflect heat back on to them in the evening and at night, so they stay warmer. Likewise, if you suffer from a lot of rain then also position them against a wall or somewhere so they are protected from the rain. However if you are growing late potatoes, then a greenhouse is an ideal location if everything else has finished growing before you put the potatoes in.

Greenhouse space is valuable and there are far better crops to grow in this precious space other than potatoes!

FEEDING & WATERING YOUR POTATOES

Potatoes are quite hungry plants and do need a lot of nutrition to grow large, healthy tubers. If you dig in plenty of organic matter such as compost or well-rotted manure before planting, then your potatoes will have a good head start in life. Do not dig in fresh manure as this will encourage wireworm and scab.

First early potatoes don't tend to need feeding, unless the soil is poor, because they are ready so quickly. You can get away with putting these in the ground and leaving them alone.

Other potato crops can benefit from a feed because they take longer to grow and exhaust the nutrients in the soil.

There is a specific potato fertilizer on the market that can be used and it comes in the form of granules which are sprinkled on top of the ground. There are slow release potato fertilizers that are put in the ground when the tubers are planted. I recommend using these if you haven't had the chance to prepare the soil or the soil is particularly weak, i.e. there are lots of large trees nearby sucking up all the nutrients.

However, it doesn't have to be used and any type of plant food such as a general liquid fertilizer or a tomato feed does the job well. Dilute and apply according to the instructions on the bottle and feed once a week.

Alternatively, use chicken manure (the pelleted variety is available in stores), comfrey tea, compost tea or any other home-made fertilizer. Many gardeners recommend a seaweed based fertilizer as it is high in micronutrients that help keep plants healthy.

Artificial fertilizers such as Miracle-Gro should be avoided. These are very high in nitrogen which will encourage plenty of leaf growth but discourage tuber growth. These artificial fertilizers have also been known to kill micro-organisms in the soil and leach natural nutrients from it. A lot of long term gardeners shy away from products like this. It is better to use a tomato food rather than use these sorts of fertilizers.

Container grown potatoes need feeding even more because they only have access to the nutrients within the container and these can quickly be exhausted. Once the leaves have appeared and you have finished earthing them up, start to feed your plants once a week.

How to Make Comfrey Tea

Comfrey tea is a great food for your potatoes (and other plants) and you get to water and feed your plants all at once! It is really easy to make out of something which many people consider to be a weed. The process is easy to follow and is pretty much the same to make nettle tea. Both these are highly nutritious and a great, organic plant food. Comfrey tends to grow in damper areas such as alongside rivers and streams though many vegetable gardeners will cultivate a small patch near their compost bins specifically for the purpose of making plant food.

Comfrey tea is very rich in both nitrogen and potassium, two of the vital nutrients for plants. The nitrogen promotes leaf growth whilst the potassium promotes the growth of the tubers. This is a good food for tomatoes, peppers, cucumbers and most berry plants as well as for your potatoes.

Before you start, a word of warning. Comfrey plants have little hairs on which can irritate the skin of some people. I strongly recommend you wear gloves and a long sleeved top to avoid skin contact with the plant. While in some people it just causes irritation and itching, in others it can cause a stronger allergic reaction.

When picking comfrey, just take the leaves off by breaking them near the main stem. Don't take too many from a single plant and you can end up with three or four "harvests" per plant during the season.

The process for making comfrey tea is very simple:

1. Get a bucket and place it away from anywhere people sit or wall past
2. Fill it between ½ and ¾ full of comfrey leaves (avoid the stems and flowers)
3. Put a brick on top of the leaves to push them down
4. Fill the container with water and then cover with a lid
5. In about 20 days the tea will be dark (and smelly) and ready to use – you can leave it up to 6 weeks and it will continue to get darker as more nutrients are drawn out of the leaves
6. Dilute the tea by at least 50% (some say 10%) before using

If you have a container with a tap on the bottom, then the liquid can be removed as it is created. Then you can keep adding leaves to the top so you have an almost continual supply of this fantastic fertilizer throughout the growing season.

Simple to make, yet highly nutritious for your plants! I'd recommend using it once a week on your potato plants applied directly to the roots.

Watering Potato Plants

Potatoes are also very thirsty plants and need a lot of water throughout the growing season. They are quite sensitive to a lack of water and it can cause problem with tuber development, meaning you get smaller potatoes at harvest time. Inconsistent watering causes all sorts of problems including split tubers, hollow hearts and more.

Potatoes are a deep root vegetable meaning that a sprinkling of water on the surface isn't really going to help their development. You have to give your potato plants a good soaking around once a week so the water goes down 12 to 18 inches and reaches the actual tubers. If it rains a lot, then you don't need to worry about watering unless your potatoes are in containers.

Make sure the water goes directly to the roots on your potato plants. Getting water on the leaves encourages the formation of fungal infections such as powdery mildew and makes a perfect environment for the dreaded blight. If you are watering in the evening, then you have to be very careful because the leaves do not have time to dry off before night. Watering in the morning means you can be a little bit more lax with your aim but you still need to be careful as water droplets on the leaves can burn the leaves during a hot day!

When the leaves start to die back, ease up on the watering though do not stop. The potatoes still need to be watered. Keep your potato bed moist, but water less frequently as the plant doesn't need the water for growing.

An irrigation system can be used to water potatoes, though ensure it is managed properly and the potatoes are not overwatered. Annoyingly, potatoes are sensitive to overwatering and too much water will cause the tubers to rot, the leaves to wilt (like under watering) and eventually kill the plant. If you are unsure whether or not to water the potatoes, stick your finger into the soil up to the second knuckle. If the soil feels damp at your finger tip then do not water otherwise give your plants a drink.

In order to conserve water, apply a mulch to your potato crop. A good mulch of something like straw, dried grass clippings or leaves will help insulate the soil and prevent water evaporation. In hotter climates this can help reduce water loss and the need for more frequent watering.

HARVESTING YOUR POTATO CROP

This is when all your hard work pays off and you finally get to see what you have produced. Because potatoes grow underground, you have no idea how they are doing until harvest time, though many of us will sneak a peek during the growing season, just to be sure things are okay!

Harvesting your potatoes is a lot of fun and really exciting. It is something your kids will enjoy too as they get really excited rooting around in the soil to find potatoes.

When to Harvest Your Potatoes
This is probably the question most often asked by people who grow potatoes. The answer depends. First early potatoes are ready when they start to flower. How noticeable the flowers are does depend on the variety, but they usually appear 10-12 weeks after planting. In some cases, the

flowers are bright and noticeable, whereas in others, the flowers are much harder to spot. You can start harvesting them then by pulling up a couple of plants as and when you need them. First early potatoes do not store as well as maincrop potatoes, so are best left in the ground unless it is really wet.

The first couple of new potato plants you harvest may not have that large a yield, but after the 12 weeks, you can reasonable expect about half a kilogram per plant (again, depending on the variety).

With second early and maincrop potatoes, when the tubers have finished growing the foliage above ground will start to turn yellow, wilt and become more and more brown and withered until it has completely died back. This is telling you that the potatoes are finished and ready to be harvested.

As your potatoes flower you may find they produce seeds which look like green cherry tomatoes. These are extremely toxic and ideally need to be removed and disposed of, particularly if you have young children or animals on your vegetable plot.

It is a bit worrying when it first happens because it can easily be confused with a disease. However, if you know when you planted your potatoes and what type you planted, then you will know if it is blight or harvest time simply from when it happens.

Cut the leaves (the haulm) off at ground level about two weeks before you are ready to harvest your maincrop potatoes. Leave the potatoes in the ground for this two weeks as it encourages the protective skin on the potatoes to 'set', making the potatoes store better. After this two weeks, lift the potatoes and store them. There isn't really any benefit to leaving them in the ground and it does increase the risk of blight, slug and pest damage.

On a sunny day (if possible), dig the potatoes up and leave them on top of the soil or on a tarp in the sun for a few hours so they can dry before you store them. On wet days, put the potatoes into aerated trays (plastic trays with holes in) and store them in a shed or greenhouse for a few days to dry before storing.

If the weather is particularly wet, then dig them up because you run the risk of them either rotting in the ground or start to sprout and grow. You certainly want to dig them up before the frosts set in because the soil can become difficult or impossible to dig!

Remove any large chunks of soil from them but don't clean them; the dirt helps protect them during storage. Whatever you do, don't wash them because then they need to be used as they will quickly start to rot.

Harvesting potatoes from containers is very easy. All you do is empty the container out on a tarp and then use your hands to look through the soil for the potatoes.

Harvesting from the ground involves a bit more effort. Potatoes are best dug up with a fork rather than a spade. With a spade you end up slicing potatoes into pieces whereas with a fork you typically just spear the odd potato, which you can still use. If you have a pitch fork, which is curved, then this is easier because it can get underneath the potatoes and lift them out. Don't worry if you do damage any potatoes as they can still be used, you just can't store them.

Approach your plant from the side, push your fork into the soil and lever the potato plant out of the ground to expose the tubers. Remove them from the plant, put the foliage to one side and put the tubers somewhere on the ground to dry. Carefully dig around and down in the area of the hole, turning the soil to find any potatoes left in the ground. If you can get them all, you will reduce the chances of unwanted plants appearing next year.

If you have mulched your potato plants, then you need to rake this off before you start harvesting. Compost the mulch and clear the soil so you can get to your potatoes easily.

The potato foliage ideally should be bagged up and disposed of or burnt. I do not recommend composting it purely because you run the risk of introducing blight spores into your compost. Although no blight may have appeared on your plant, the spores could be present so just to be on the safe side don't compost it.

Don't try to harvest your potatoes by pulling at the foliage as you are unlikely to get many, if any, potatoes up. You will get a handful of leaves and will still need to dig them out. If you don't want to dig out potatoes, then I recommend you grow them in containers!

You need to sort your potatoes into two piles after they have dried. One pile contains the unblemished potatoes, meaning those with no holes in it, no bruising and no damage. These are stored for later use.

The second pile is the potatoes that have been damaged so those with wire worm or slug damage, those speared while digging them up or any other damage. Storing damaged potatoes will lead to them rotting which will then damage the rest of your harvest. These potatoes are to be used first before using the undamaged potatoes – just cut out any damaged areas.

Harvesting Blighted Potatoes

If the potatoes have been attacked by late potato blight, harvesting is slightly different. Cut the haulm (foliage) off at ground level, bag it up and dispose of it. Then leave the potatoes in the ground for 2-3 weeks. Put some beer traps around the rows of potatoes to catch slugs and prevent them from damaging the tubers. The potatoes are left in the ground to reduce the risk of blight spores landing on the potatoes which will then cause blight while they are in storage.

If the blight is particularly bad, wash the potatoes in a bucket of water with a few drops of washing up liquid to remove any blight spores. When dried thoroughly, the potatoes should store ok, but store in a single layer and check them regularly for signs of blight.

STORING POTATOES

Once you have dug your potatoes up you will need to store them. Potatoes need to be stored in a cool, dark, dry place with good air circulation such as a garage or basement. Do not wash the potatoes before storing them but gently brush off any excess soil. Check all potatoes before storing them and make sure there is no damage. Any damaged potatoes need using over the next couple of weeks.

Ideally, potatoes need to be stored at between 7-10C or 45-50F. Make sure that wherever you store them is frost free as they will not tolerate being frozen. Do not store them in your refrigerator either as they turn sweet and their consistency changes.

Do not store your potatoes in plastic containers as this encourages the build-up of moisture as the potatoes "sweat" which will cause them to rot. Also, do not store them in any air tight container.

Potatoes are best stored in baskets, cardboard boxes, paper bags or hessian sacks. The latter are my favorite because they are perforated which allows for air flow around the potatoes. Alternatively, you can find a chip shop or other fast food restaurant that uses fresh potatoes and ask them for their old potato bags (which they often throw away) and store yours in there.

A good alternative for smaller harvests are the large paper bags you get from fast food stores with your food in. The stronger ones with handles are ideal for storing potatoes in. I collect paper bags like this from supermarkets and fast food restaurants throughout the year, ready to store my potato harvest in. The smaller bags are good for storing those you are going to use in the kitchen whereas bigger sacks are good for longer term storage. Plastic mushroom or bread trays are also very good for storing potatoes as they have plenty of holes and the potatoes are not stacked on top of each other.

When storing your potatoes, do not pack them into the container too tightly. Air must be able to circulate between the potatoes to keep them fresh. Remember to store them out of the light as sunlight will make them turn green and become inedible.

Avoid storing your potatoes with onions as they emit gasses which will cause both crops to rot.

When stored correctly, potatoes will last for several months and even up to six months in optimal conditions. Remember that later cropping potatoes store far better than the early varieties.

Potatoes stored in a too cold environment will convert their starch to sugar. This means that when you cook them they develop a brown color and taste a bit peculiar. To reduce this effect, remove any potatoes you want to use from storage a couple of days in advance and store in the dark at room temperature. This converts the sugar back to starch so they taste better.

If your potatoes are exposed to light and become green, then you need to check it carefully. If the green penetrates deep inside the potato, throw the whole thing away. In many cases it will just be on the skin so you can peel it off and still use the rest of the potato.

Sometimes your potatoes will start to sprout in storage. So long as the tuber itself hasn't started to shrivel they can still be used. Just remove the sprouts and use the potato as normal.

Storing your harvest is very important and you need to take care to do it correctly. Well stored your potatoes will last for several months so it can be worth planting a lot if you are going to store them properly. Remember, maincrop varieties store the best!

DEALING WITH POTATO BLIGHT

Blight is the scourge of any potato grower and once it has taken hold on your plants there is no getting rid of it. Late blight affects all members of the potato family, including tomatoes and can destroy your crop in as little as ten days. It is a fungal disease caused by the spores of *Phytophthora Infestans*. If you remember hearing about the Irish Potato famine in the 1840s which killed over a million people, blight caused the famine!

Blight is particularly prevalent during warm and humid weather, usually striking from mid to late July, though in a warm year it can start as early as June. The spores blow in on the wind and infect your plants. Until blight has started to damage your plants there is no way of knowing whether or not they have been contaminated.

Blight affects outdoor crops the most but it can also infect greenhouse crops if the conditions are humid. Blight is brought into a greenhouse by the wind through the open doors and windows or on your clothes/boots as you walk inside. There is no way of avoiding blight if it strikes, you just have to undertake damage limitation.

Blight starts with dark brown blotches on the leaves, as shown in the picture above. These are most often found towards the tips and edges. If you look carefully you will see white fungal spores developing on the underside of the leaves. As the blight spreads so the leaves and stem will yellow, blacken and rot, eventually causing the plant to collapse.

The spores spread on the wind and as it takes hold they will spread through to your other plants (one reason why spacing is important – it helps to slow the spread of disease). The spores can even wash into the soil and then infect the tubers. This causes a reddish brown rot just below the surface of the skin which spreads towards the middle of the potato.

The fungal spores can remain in the soil or in infected plant material (tubers or leaves) which are left on the ground or in the compost heap. If blight does strike, then all infected plant material needs to be removed and destroyed otherwise you are leaving blight spores in the ground. Crop rotation is important because it helps avoid the build-up of blight spores and helps reduce the risk of infection. Some seasoned gardeners recommend spraying infected areas with a diluted solution of Jeyes fluid, which not only kills blight spores, but also kills pests such as wire-worm. While I have not tried this myself as I am unsure on the effect on beneficial organisms (I can't imagine it is good), they plant potatoes in the same area year after year without any negative effects.

As there is so little you can do to save a blighted plant, precaution is the watch word. You can buy chemical sprays to use on infected plants but these are expensive and do not destroy the blight, just delay it killing your crop. If you are going to do this, spray before blight starts with an approved fungicide at around the start of June, particularly if the weather is wet. Then spray again when the new growth appears. Follow the instructions on the packet and it may hold off blight long enough for you to harvest the potatoes.

It is important that you start with healthy, disease free seed potatoes. This is one reason why you don't use store bought potatoes; you have no guarantees they are blight free.

There are blight resistant varieties of potatoes you can buy but remember that they are resistant, not immune! If they are going to get blight then they will get it, but later than a non-resistant variety. Some blight resistant varieties you can buy are Sarpo Mira, Kifli, Blue Danube, Orla (a first early), Shone and Sharpo Axona. There are others available and you should buy these if there is a blight problem in your area.

Because of when blight strikes you can usually avoid it by planting just first early potatoes. They are typically harvested before blight starts to take hold. The downside of this is that they don't store as well as late crop potatoes, but it is worth doing if blight regularly strikes your crop so you at least get to harvest your potatoes. On the plus side, the space freed up by harvesting your potatoes can be used for a second crop for a later harvest.

You can help to avoid the onset of blight by ensuring you leave sufficient space between the plants. This allows the air to flow around the leaves which helps them to dry out quicker after getting wet. This will slow the spread of blight and make a less blight-friendly environment. Also, watering in the morning and at the base of the plants helps because the leaves don't get wet. If you have to water in the evening, which many people do due to work commitments, avoid getting water on the leaves as this will encourage blight to take hold. Most of us water potatoes by spraying the leaves, but that creates the damp environment the fungal spores love.

If blight is a problem in your area then start spraying your potatoes with a protective fungicide before you see the signs of blight, i.e. from about

June. If wet weather is forecast, then it is important that you spray and that you spray every two or three weeks to protect new growth. Check the instructions on the box for exact details of how often to spray.

Should you see signs of blight then remove all infected plant material and destroy it. Pick up any fallen leaves and dispose of them properly. Do not add them to your compost heap as the spores will live on and then be spread all over your vegetable garden when you use your compost. This infected material is best burnt or bagged up and put in the trash.

If your plants have already developed tubers and blight strikes later in the growing season, then you should cut away all the stems and foliage to about an inch off the ground. Leave the potatoes in the ground and do not dig them up. After two or three weeks of leaving the soil undisturbed (don't water either as that will carry the spores into the ground) the spores should be killed off and you can lift your crop without infecting it. If it rains a lot during this time, you are better off digging up the potatoes, washing them, drying them and storing them otherwise the rain will wash the blight into the soil and the tubers.

Any potato plants that appear the next spring should be dug up and destroyed as they probably going to contain blight spores and will infect your new season crop early on in the year.

Avoid planting tomatoes anywhere near to potatoes as blight infects both plants. If your tomatoes get infected your potatoes may avoid it, but if they are near to each other then both crops will be destroyed.

Getting blight is truly soul destroying when you see your hard work destroyed but if you take sensible precautions and take action as soon as you see the first signs you will still be able to harvest some potatoes. Plant your maincrop early or just plant first earlies and you should be able to avoid the worst of blight, if not avoid it completely. Most importantly though, keep a close eye on your plants and watch for any signs of infection.

COMMON POTATO PESTS & DISEASES

Potatoes are generally hardy plants and suffer less problems than many other plants. They can tough out most environments, though blight is probably the most serious problem they face, as you learnt in the previous chapter.

Some of the other common problems will be discussed now to help you either prevent it from happening or to spot the first signs and prevent it from spreading. Be aware that there are many other diseases but as a home-grower, you are very unlikely to ever see them. If there are farmers growing commercial potato crops in your area, then you have more of a chance of encountering some of the unusual pests and diseases, but in general farmers now are buying certified disease free potatoes to avoid crop loss.

Aphids

These can be problem for potatoes in high numbers, but generally, do little damage, being more of a threat to other plants. However, the danger with aphids is that they can infect potato plants with other diseases, though this is more of a risk if you live in an area where potatoes are grown commercially.

Aphids can be picked off by hand or sprayed off with water. Insecticidal soap sprays are an effective treatment against this pest.

Black Dot

This is a mild disease, caused by the fungus *Colletotrichum coccodes* that is commonly found in store bought, pre-packed potatoes. Symptoms are visible later in the season on the stems and roots, though it does not necessarily lead to diseased tubers. It can cause the leaves to wilt and the plant to die back early. Black dot is found across the world where potatoes are grown.

Infected tubers can be unblemished or have light brown blemishes on it, but with small black dots. As the tubers grow, dark brown patches can develop. On red potatoes, these lesions look silvery so this disease can be confused with silver scurf, though the black dots are visible if you look carefully with a magnifying glass.

This disease is found in infected tubers, though can be introduced through contaminated soil. In storage, warm, humid conditions encourage this disease.

This virus can survive in the ground for up to seven years, so long crop rotation (3 or 4 years) can help reduce the risk of this. Keeping your potato bed clear of weeds can help reduce the risk of this disease too.

Some varieties that are resistant to this disease include:

- Eva
- Keuka Gold
- NorDonna
- Norwis

There are fungicides available to treat this, though many are not licenced for home use.

Blackleg and Bacterial Soft Rot

This is a common bacterial disease that causes a black rot at the base of the stem. It is caused by the bacteria *Pectobacterium atrosepticum* and appears from June onwards. It is worse in wet years and only infects potatoes. The leaves turn yellow or pale green and those at the top of the plant can curl inwards. The tubers, if they form, have grey, brown or even rotten flesh.

If you see signs of this disease, remove and destroy infected plants. Like many potato diseases, it thrives in warm, damp conditions and poorly drained soils. There are no chemical controls available for this disease.

There are some resistant varieties available, including:

- Charlotte
- Pixie
- Saxon
- Vales Sovereign

As a home gardener, the most likely way that this will be introduced into your vegetable garden is through infected tubers. If you buy certified disease free seed potatoes, then you are much less likely to encounter this disease. Blackleg is found across Europe and North America.

Black Scurf and Stem Canker

This fungal disease, *Rhizoctonia solani*, causes stem canker, damping off and tuber growth distortion. It can be soil or seed borne and survives for a long time in the soil either on crop debris of volunteer potatoes left over from previous years.

When a plant is infected, the roots and stems develop reddish brown patches called cankers that, on a stem, are similar to blackleg. On the stem base, brown, slightly sunken lesions with defined edges will develop. The tubers only have superficial markings on them, but this can be scraped off easily enough.

There are no resistant varieties available, but seed potatoes are usually free from this. Planting in well-drained seed beds and using crop rotation will help prevent this disease.

Colorado Potato Beetle

Colorado Potato Beetles, *Leptinotarsa decemlineata*, are a major problem for growers in the United States, having first been recorded in 1859. It arrived in continental Europe in Bordeaux, France, in 1922, but has not, as of yet, made its way to the United Kingdom. However, with climate change, there is a risk of it travelling to the UK and other countries.

It is probably one of the best known potato pests and known for not just attacking potatoes, but also tomatoes, aubergines (eggplant) and peppers. Adult beetles and their larvae can strip plants of leaves and destroy an entire crop.

The adults are dome shaped and around 0.5" long, yellow in color with five black stripes on each wing cover. It is notorious for developing resistance to insecticides and it is vital that any sighting of it is reported and treated immediately. The females lay clusters of bright yellow/orange oval shaped eggs on the underside of potato leaves.

The larvae are orange with a black head and two rows of black spots on their body. Young larvae are a darker red and as they age the color lightens and can be a pinkish color.

This is a challenging pest to deal with and the best results come from using a combination of different management tactics.

The Colorado potato beetle emerges in the spring and look for plants to use as hosts if there are no potatoes around. This includes common weeds such as nightshade and ground cherry. As these weeds are a food source for this beetle, removing the weeds starves the pest out and they either die out or move on.

The adult beetle emerges in mid-summer, so planting early maturing varieties means the plants are harvested and removed from the ground before the beetles are searching for food. The downside of this is that early varieties do not store as well and are not as large as maincrop potatoes. Alternatively, growing potatoes every other year can help reduce the population, but there must be no potatoes growing within a radius of 1/4 to 1/2 mile and temperatures are not too warm, otherwise the beetle can survive.

Adult beetles can be handpicked off the plants, which is effective for the home-grower, but not so much for the commercial or larger scale grower. Drop the adult beetles into a bucket filled with soapy water to kill them. Check the undersides of leaves for the yellow/orange eggs and remove or crush them.

As the adults fly, they can migrate into your garden, so you need to check your plants regularly.

Sadly, this beetle has few natural enemies to prey on it. Stink bugs and lady birds will eat the eggs of the Colorado potato beetle. The fungus, Beauveria bassiana, kills both the larvae and adults, though natural enemies have very little impact on the numbers of this beetle.

Synthetic pesticides such as carbaryl, cypermethrin, deltamethrin, lambda cyhalothrin, imidacloprid, permethrin, and pyrethrins are not effective as the Colorado potato beetle has developed resistance to them. If you use any other pesticide and it doesn't seem to be killing the beetle, immediately switch to one with a different active ingredient.

The beetle is not, as of yet, resistant or spinosad or azadirachtin (neem oil). Neem oil, mixed with a little mild dish soap is effective for a couple of days though requires regular application and is not as effective against larger larvae and adults. Spinosad is made from a soil bacterium, Saccharopolyspora spinosa, and is effective against the beetle for up to 10-14 days.

Dry Rot

Dry rot is a major problem for commercial potato growers, being one of the main cause of crop loss after harvest across the United States and Europe. Great Britain estimates it affects about 1% of tubers, which is a lot of potatoes if you consider the quantity grown. It is caused by four Fusarium species and is more common in warm sandy soils. As a home grower, this is much less likely to be an issue for you, though if you live in a rural, potato growing area, then potentially, this could be a problem.

Dry rot develops around a wound in the potato and dehydrates in concentric wrinkles with a white, fluffy, mouldy growth. Inside the tuber, you can find more of the mould growing as well as brown rotting.

This pathogen is soil borne but can also be transmitted through infected seed potatoes. It is not seen immediately when the potatoes are harvested, but develops as the potatoes are in storage, usually becoming noticeable after the end of the year of harvest.

The risk of this disease can be minimized with longer crop rotation plans and by leaving plenty of time for the potatoes to cure fully before storage.

Dickeya

This bacteria causes tuber soft rot and can be found in most countries in one form or another. It is less common in the UK and potato growers have taken steps to minimize and prevent its introduction. This disease causes wilting and stem rot as well as rotting the tubers themselves. It is found across the world though in Australia, South America and the USA.

Early Blight

Also known as early blight, this is a soil based fungal disease, *Alternaria Solani*, found across the world. It is common in warm, wet weather and does not normally kill the plants. It does cause significant leaf loss which can lead to reduction in yield of up to 30%. It infects any member of the potato family, including tomatoes.

This blight is usually found on mature plants, rather than on new growth. The older, lower leaves are usually the first to be infected and dark, brown spots will start to appear. As the disease progresses, these increase in size and become angular in shape. The often end up looking like a target and this disease is referred to as 'target spot' in some areas. The leaf will eventually yellow and die, but still remain attached to the plant. In some infections, the stems will have black or dark brown spots on them.

The tubers are infected with this blight and end up with dark gray to purple lesions with raised edges. Inside, the flesh is dry, brown and leathery or corky. In advanced stages, the flesh looks like it has been soaked in water and takes on a yellow/green color.

The spores of this fungus lives in the soil and in infected plant debris, i.e. in infected tubers, leaves and roots. The spores spread on the wind or by splashes caused by rain, then enter the plant through wounds including those caused by insect damage.

Resistant varieties of potato are available, with late maturing potatoes having a greater level of resistance than early potatoes. Water at the base of the plant, rather than the leaves and rotate your crops.

Some early blight resistant potatoes include:

- Accent
- Acoustic
- Cara
- Jazzy
- Nicola
- Setanta
- Sarpo Axona
- Sarpo Mira
- Setanta
- Valor
- Vitabella

Eelworm

There are two types of eelworm that affect potatoes, the golden and the white. Eelworms are also known as the Potato Cyst Nematode and has two different Latin names; *Globodera rostochiensis* (golden nematode) and *Globodera pallida* (white nematode). However, they are also sometimes referred to by the previous Latin names, *Heterodera rostochiensis* and *Heterodera pallida*.

This infection is quite difficult to diagnose, but when your plant is infected with this the growth will appear stunted and the yield is reduced. The leaves on plants with severe infections turn yellow and the foliage dies back early, usually just in the areas infected with eelworm. Eelworms do not damage the tubers, they only feed on the roots where the cysts containing eelworm eggs can be seen with a magnifying glass.

Eelworms are not airborne or waterborne and in fact, they barely more, shifting by not much more than a metre in a single growing season. They are introduced into the soil either through infected seed potatoes or on soil brought in from elsewhere, usually on footwear.

Unfortunately, there is no treatment for eelworm. Buying certified disease free potatoes ensures you do not accidentally bring it into your garden. Good crop rotation will prevent this pest building up in the soil, though if you do get an infestation then you must not grow potatoes in that area for a minimum of six years, though eelworm can persist in the soil for as much as ten years. There are eelworm resistant varieties of potatoes, but like blight resistant varieties, they are not immune! Some resistant varieties include:

- Cara
- Kestrel
- Nicola
- Maris Piper
- Swift

Removing and destroying all foliage and roots at the end of the growing season will help minimize the risk of this disease building up in the soil. In general, first and second earlies avoid eelworm damage as they are ready to harvest before the damage takes place.

Flea Beetle

These are tiny, black or brown insects that chew small holes in plant leaves. Typically, they attack young plants and they are not fussy about which plants they attack.

Cover young plants with fabric to protect them and rotate your crops to prevent this pest building up in the soil. Encouraging your plants to outgrow the flea beetle is the best treatment. Use a high nitrogen feed to help the plants grow plenty of foliage and resist the beetle. In serious infestations, they can cause a lot of damage to young plants.

Spinosad is effective in treating this pest whereas neem oil is not. Fungal agents containing *Beauveria bassiana* and *Metarhizium brunneum*, are effective, causing the beetles to dry out and die.

Mosaic Virus

The mosaic viruses can vary in severity from no damage to the leaves (latent virus) through to significant distortion of the leaves. These diseases are less common in for the home grower as generally we use disease free seed potatoes. However, if there is commercial potato crops in your area, this disease can find its way into the home-growers crop.

Identifying this disease can be difficult because there are several symptoms and they look similar to other diseases, though a common symptom is a mottling or mild mosaic on the leaves. There are no symptoms on the tubers and it is transmitted either through infected tubers or, with some varieties of the virus, through aphids. Spraying against aphids can reduce the risk of this disease in areas prone to it.

Any infected plant material needs to be destroyed. It must not be composted. Keep the area around the plants free of weeds and disinfect gardening tools between uses to prevent spreading this disease.

Pink Rot

Pink rot, *Phytophthora erythroseptica*, can be devastating in hot dry years, though it does require a wet soil in order to infect potatoes. It does not affect the foliage, though late in the growing season it can cause wilt. The rotting tubers can be spotted sometimes when they are lifted because the soil sticks a little too firmly to the surface of the tuber. The tubers have a distinctive sweet smell and if you squeeze the tuber, it will ooze a clear, colorless liquid. When cut, the flesh may appear okay initially, but will turn pink and then dark brownor black in an hour or two.

This is not common f or the home-grower and more often found on a commercial scale. Buying certified disease free seed potatoes helps avoid this disease. Long crop rotation is another way to tackle this disease.

Potato Blackleg

This is disease is caused by a bacteria *Erwinia carotovora* var *atrospetica* that is common in the UK and is usually caused by infected tubers. This is one reason why you should always buy seed potatoes from reputable sources and not plant potatoes bought from supermarkets.

This disease starts early in the growing season, with it not being unusual for plants to show signs of infection from the middle of June. The leaves start to turn yellow some time before the potatoes are mature and the leaves turn inwards. The base of the stem will turn a black or dark brown color as it starts to rot. Eventually, the infection spreads up the plant, causing it to completely collapse. Infected tubers will have a grey or brown slimy rot inside them or may have completely rotted away.

As this disease normally comes from infected tubers, it will usually just affect a single plant; the one grown from the infected tuber. Luckily, it does not easily pass between plants. It does not persist in the soil or spread well between plants.

If you see signs of this disease, then remove and destroy any infected plants and improve the soil drainage.

Potato Leafroll Virus

This was once the most commonly found virus in potato seed stocks, causing the greatest yield loss. It is now less common and not often seen by the home-grower unless they live in an area where potatoes are grown commercially.

In the first year of infection, symptoms are slight and can be missed. These are usually a slight rolling of the leaves and a reddish orange tinge on the upper leaves. In the second year of infection, the bottom leaves may roll and the leaves become dry and brittle, feeling like paper.

As this disease is transmitted my aphids, which, once infected with the virus are infective for the rest of their lives, it can transmit from commercial crops to home-grown crops.

Disease free potatoes and controlling the aphids will minimize the risk of this disease. Any infected plant material must not be composted and needs to be destroyed.

Potato Scab

Common scab leaves odd lesions, like cork, on the skin of potatoes. Although this has no effect on the taste and can easily be peeled off, it does reduce the time the potato can be stored. It makes the potato less visually appealing, but this is only a problem if you enter vegetable growing competitions.

Scab is caused by a bacteria called Streptomyces scabies and is, interestingly enough, not just restricted to potatoes. It can affect any vegetable that forms under the soil such as radishes and beetroot. There are no above ground signs of infection; you only notice when you dig the potatoes up.

This disease mainly occurs where water is scarce as the plant is developing. If you can, grow potatoes in a moist, well-drained soil with lots of well-rotted organic matter. It is common when manure has been used on the potato bed but it hasn't fully rotted down before being dug in. Scab is made worse if the soil is very alkaline, so do not add any lime to a potato bed for at least a year before the potatoes are planted.

Improve the soil and make sure you use well-rotted compost and manure. Regularly water your potatoes throughout the growing season and ensure they do not dry out. If you do end up with some infected tubers, then use those first and do not store them.

There is no chemical solution to scab so if it is prevalent in your area, grow a scab resistant variety such as:

- Accent
- Arran Pilot
- Desiree
- King Edwards
- Nicola

Slugs and Snails

These are a common problem, though slugs are much more of an issue for potatoes than snails. The latter will damage the foliage whereas small slugs live in the soil and attack the tubers. This is obviously difficult to spot until harvest time.

Unfortunately, slug damage usually renders the potato inedible as they dig into the potato and start eating the inside, turning the flesh brown around the areas they have tunnelled into.

If you spot any sign of slugs, then you should take steps to kill them off such as slug pellets or beer traps. Whilst there are other solutions on the market such as copper tape, coffee grounds and egg shells these aren't particularly effective. If you are using slug pellets, be careful which type you use as they do have a very negative impact on beneficial wildlife such as hedgehogs and frogs. Sheep wool has recently been discovered to be very effective against slugs, as has thorny brambles placed around plants.

However, much of the damage to the tubers is not done by slugs that live on the soil, but by slugs that spend most of their lives under the ground. Above ground slugs and snails will eat some of the leaves, but rarely enough to impact the developing tubers.

One solution to the problem is to grow early potatoes that are lifted before slugs become a problem. Another method of reducing this damage is by using blood, fish and bone as a fertilizer instead of manure. As slug damage usually starts in August, lifting and storing potatoes early, rather than leaving them in the ground, can reduce the losses to slugs.

There are some slug resistant varieties such as:

- Charlotte
- Estima
- Golden Wonder
- Kestrel
- Sante
- Wilja

An old gardener's trick, that I do not know if it works or not as I have never tried it, is to put a single slug pellet underneath each seed potato during planting. It is something old gardeners swear by as an effective method of prevent slug damage.

Wireworm

Wireworm is a pest that lives underground so you won't notice the damage until you dig up your potatoes. This pest is the larva of the click beetle, which themselves do very little damage to vegetables. As well as potatoes, this pest will also attach carrots and tomatoes and other vegetables. They are more common in ground that recently had grass growing on it as the wireworms feed on grass roots too.

If your potato plants have been infected, each tuber will have several holes in it. The holes will usually have a black edge with a larger brown ring around it. Unfortunately, this does make the potato more susceptible to infection with other diseases.

Because the tubers are being attacked directly, the longer you leave your potatoes in the ground the more they will be affected by wireworms. If you are unsure if it is wireworms or slugs damaging your potatoes cut the tuber in to quarters and you will see signs of tunnelling if it is wireworm.

Wireworms can live in the soil for up to five years so if you get a serious infestation you will have to avoid growing potatoes in that area for that length of time. They prefer a cool, moist soil and dig deeper if the weather becomes too warm and dry.

There isn't any treatment for wireworm and very little signs that they are in the ground before you harvest your potatoes.

However, if you give the soil a good digging, down to around a foot deep after the harvest this will kill the wireworm larvae as they don't like being on the surface and it exposes them to predators. There are no wireworm resistant variety of potato currently available, though circumstantial evidence does say that King Edward, Nadine and Maris Piper are less likely to be affected. Growing first/second earlies can reduce the damage caused by wireworm.

THE BEST & MOST UNUSUAL POTATO VARIETIES

There are around 5,000 different varieties of potatoes at the time of writing, so obviously I'm not going to list them all here. What I will do is list some of the most common uses for potatoes and the best potatoes available for that use. Which potatoes you can buy will depend on your area, but if you search around online you will be able to find most varieties. Remember to buy from certified suppliers to ensure you get disease free seed potatoes.

Which potato variety you choose will depend on what you want to use it for. A variety that makes great mashed potato may not be good for roasting. There are general purpose potatoes which are a good bet for most home growers.

Before choosing your variety (or varieties – I usually plant 3 or 4 varieties each year) you need to decide when you want to harvest your crop. If you want them earlier in the year then first earlies are for you, though if you want a later crop you may choose a maincrop variety.

You also need to decide how long you want to store your potatoes for – first earlies do not store well whereas maincrop potatoes do. You also need to decide what you want to use your potatoes for as a roasting potato may not be good for mashing or baking or boiling. If you try to boil a potato that is good for roasting, you end up disappointed as certain varieties are best cooked in certain ways. If you are unsure of what you want to do with your potatoes, then buy a general purpose potato which will be a good all-rounder no matter how you use it.

Also think about whether or not you need any disease resistance. Is your area prone to blight, slugs, wireworm or any other problems which could affect your potato crop? If so, then you want to buy a disease resistant variety.

Most people plant a variety of potatoes such as some first earlies, second earlies, maincrop and late so that they have a continuous harvest throughout the year. I personally stick to first earlies due to blight problems but having recently moved, there may not be blight issues in this area so I could grow other varieties again.

Typically, you will plant some general purpose potatoes, some good for roasting and some salad potatoes. Ultimately it depends on how you use your potatoes and the space available to you, but typically I'll plant a few of each type of tuber so I have a nice variety. To save you buying lots of different varieties you can buy a few and then swap them with other vegetable growers.

Certified seed potatoes are the best for you to buy because you know they are disease free and you won't be introducing problems into your garden. Although some people buy and plant store bought potatoes you have no guarantee they are disease free.

Slug Resistant Potato Varieties

The following varieties have been bred to be resistant to damage by slugs and are great if you have a slug problem where you live:

- Arran Pilot
- Blue Kestrel
- Cara
- Estima
- Kestrel
- Pentland Javelin
- Sarpo Axona
- Swift
- Wilja

Disease Resistant Potato Varieties

These varieties have some resistance to the disease listed but note that does not mean they are immune.

- Accent – scab resistant
- Arran Pilot – scab resistant
- Cara – blight resistant
- Charlotte – blight and slug resistant
- Desiree – scab resistant
- Golden Wonder – scab resistant
- King Edward – scab resistant
- Markies – blight resistant
- Nicola – scab resistant
- Sarpo Axona – excellent blight resistance
- Sarpo Mira – excellent blight resistance
- Setanta – good blight resistance
- Valor – blight resistant

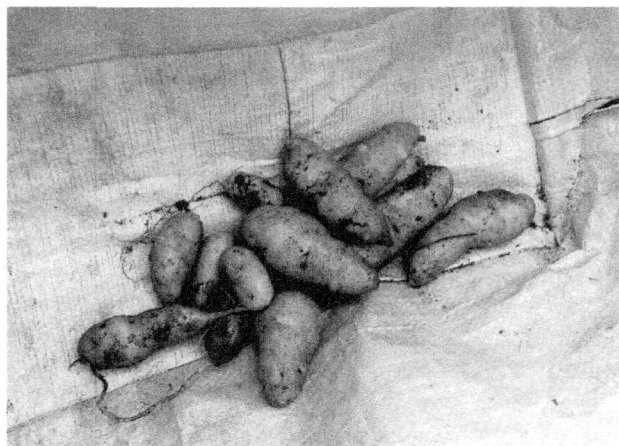

Best Potatoes for Storing

Early varieties of potatoes and salad potatoes are not good for storing though maincrop varieties will usually store for several months if stored correctly. Here are some of the best varieties for storing.

- Pink Fir Apple – a salad potato which will store for up to three months
- Kerr's Pink
- Majestic
- Maris Piper
- Sarpo Axona – stores for four to six months

Best Salad and New Potatoes

If you like boiled new potatoes, then early potatoes are the best to use. Although there are maincrop varieties available the early potatoes will always produce a better crop and taste better. Some good varieties I can recommend include:

- Arran Pilot
- Nicola
- Charlotte (very nice firm potatoes)
- Lady Christl
- Anya
- Jersey Royal (very popular though usually sold as International Kidney due to trademark issues)
- Pink Fir Apple

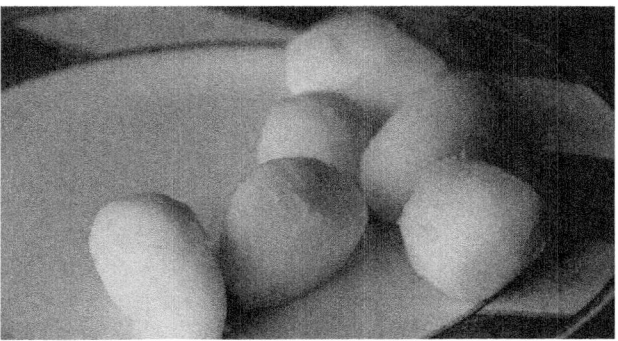

Best Potatoes for Boiling and Steaming

The best varieties for boiling are either maincrop or second early varieties. Red Duke of York is a good first early for boiling but some second earlies that work well are:

- Kestrel
- Maris Peer
- Nadine
- Wilja
- Estima

Some maincrop varieties that are great for boiling include:

- Celine
- King Edward
- Maris Piper
- Arran Victory
- Maxine

Best Potatoes for Baking

It is very important you choose the right variety if you are going to bake your potatoes as the wrong variety will either not cook properly or fall to pieces. You need a large potato that will retain its shape, cooks evenly and softens nicely when cooked. Some of the best baking potatoes are:

- Nadine
- Maxine
- Maris Peer
- Maris Piper
- King Edward (though the potatoes can be a little small)

Best Potatoes for Mashing

Second early potatoes such as Kestral and Wilja make for excellent mashing potatoes as does Vivaldi. From maincrop potatoes the following potatoes are highly recommended:

- Arran Victory
- King Edward
- Maris Piper

Best Potatoes for Chips (Frying)

For the best chip or fried potato you are looking for a potato that is dry but fluffs up on the inside whilst crisping up on the outside.

Popular varieties include Desiree and King Edward. However, the majority of British fish and chip shops who produce tons of fried potatoes each day use Maris Piper potatoes and they do make fantastic chips (fries).

Best Potatoes for Roasting

Roast potatoes are one of the favorite ways to cook potatoes, being a particular popular dish in England. A roast potato needs to be one that fluffs up well when cooked and is soft on the inside. There are many varieties you can use but the best by far is King Edward.

Other popular varieties which work well are:
- Arran Victory
- Kerr's Pink
- Maris Piper
- Sarpo Axona

My favorite recipe for making roast potatoes is as follows:
1. Put a roasting tin with your choice of fat in to the oven at 200C/400F (180C in a fan oven or gas mark 6) (goose fat works really well)
2. Peel your potatoes and cut into even sized pieces (not too big otherwise the middle will not be cooked before the outside burns)
3. Bring the potatoes to the boil in salted water
4. When the water starts to boil turn the heat down and simmer for two minutes
5. Drain the potatoes in a colander and shake well to fluff up the outside
6. Sprinkle a couple of teaspoons of flour or fine semolina over them and shake well to ensure they are thinly coated and evenly covered
7. Carefully put the potatoes into the roasting tin – watch out as the hot oil will spit
8. Roll the potatoes over and ensure they are in a single layer – they need to be covered with oil on all sides
9. Roast for 15 minutes then turn before roasting for another 15 minutes and turning again
10. Leave for another 10 to 20 minutes until they are golden and crisp – don't worry if the color is uneven, it will be
11. Serve and enjoy!

An alternative I use is I parboil the potatoes, then spray them with oil and add some dried parsley or rosemary and some salt. They are then shaken up and cooked in the oven with oil or in an air fryer and they come out absolutely delicious!

Best Potatoes for a Christmas Harvest

Growing potatoes for Christmas has become extremely popular and you can now buy seed potatoes in late summer which will, supposedly, produce a crop ready for Christmas dinner. These have been cold stored to prevent them from sprouting and are planted in August or September.

In reality though, unless you live in a warm area this doesn't really happen. The potatoes sprout very quickly as the soil is warm in August. The potatoes are ready towards the end of October at which time most of us are starting to experience frosts so the foliage needs cutting back (remember to mark where your potatoes are though otherwise you will struggle to find them).

Depending on the weather you may need to lift and store the potatoes as you can find there is too much wet weather and you run the risk of your crop rotting. Good varieties to grow include:

- Charlotte
- Maris Peer
- Nicola
- Rooster

GROWING CHRISTMAS POTATOES

Growing potatoes for Christmas or Thanksgiving has become popular as many home-growers like to grow as much of their festive meals as possible. These cold stored tubers are available from specialist suppliers in July and August. They are seed potatoes from the previous year that have been held back to plant in the summer. Be aware that these are very popular and can quickly sell out, so get your orders in early.

First and second early potatoes are good as they do not need chitting and can go straight into the soil. You can store seed potatoes bought in the spring in your fridge for summer planting. Be aware that these will chit and need to be planted carefully so as not to damage the shoots. Potatoes harvested from that year cannot be used as they have a long period of dormancy after harvesting and will not produce tubers by winter.

It will take around 12 weeks from planting to harvest and should be lifted around the time of the first frosts as the cold will kill the foliage. Alternatively, potatoes can be planted in bags in a frost-free greenhouse or cool conservatory for a Christmas harvest.

Growing Christmas Potatoes Indoors

When growing potatoes for Christmas indoors, you need a large container. Potato bags are ideal, but any container that is at least 30cm/12" deep with drainage holes in the base is suitable.

Add 10cm/4" of compost to the container if it is 30cm/12" deep. Fill larger containers half full with compost. As the potatoes grow and the foliage appears, earth up the potatoes as normal until the soil level is within 5cm/2" of the top of the container. This makes watering easier as the soil does not wash away. Water well and feed regularly.

In October to early November, the foliage will die down and then can be removed.

Leave the tubers in the containers and keep the compost mostly dry until you need them.

Growing Christmas Potatoes Outdoors

Grow potatoes as you would normally, planting in August and protecting against blight and slugs. When the foliage dies down towards the end of September or October, cut it down at ground level.

If you have a light soil in a sheltered area, pile earth over the rows of potatoes and cover with straw to insulate the tubers until Christmas.

In colder areas, or areas with wet, heavy soil, lift the tubers at the end of October and store them in soil or coarse sand in a frost free area. If the ground freezes, it makes it very difficult to get the potatoes out of the ground until the ground has defrosted in the spring. Plus, if the start of winter is very wet, it can rot the tubers or encourage pest damage.

Storing the potatoes in your fridge or in bags in a cool shed works, but it makes the skins harden and you lose the 'new-potato' taste and texture.

If you have a greenhouse or polytunnel that isn't otherwise being used, growing Christmas potatoes in them is a good idea. Heating a greenhouse just to grow these potatoes is not really cost effective, but if you have other plants in it and some spare space, it is worth putting a few bags of potatoes in.

Be aware that potatoes grown outside in summer and autumn are more prone to potato blight, whereas those grown indoors are not usually at risk.

If a frost is forecast, fleece your potato plants to protect the foliage. This will work in light frosts, but when the temperature plummets a lot, a fleece is not generally adequate protection. Hopefully, the potatoes will be finished before the frosts hit.

Growing Christmas/Thanksgiving potatoes is good fun and something more gardeners are doing. It is nice to combine these with home-grown cabbage, cauliflower, carrots and broccoli for your festive meal. I don't know about you, but I love being able to make a festive meal even more special by serving food that I have grown.

GROWING SWEET POTATOES

Sweet potatoes are a great variety of potato to grow. They are becoming more popular as they are considered better for you than normal potatoes as they contain a lot of vitamins. Typically, sweet potatoes are eating around Thanksgiving in America but make a great addition to the dinner table being packed with calcium, iron, vitamins A and C and other vital minerals. They store well and are not too difficult to grow so definitely worth a try.

Sweet potatoes are a tropical vegetable with a long growing season. They need four or five months of warmth to develop the large sweet roots we enjoy. Sweet potatoes thrive when it is too hot for most other vegetables.

They can be grown further north though they are a bit more challenging. Sweet potatoes are extremely tender and the plants will die in even a light frost. They refuse to grow in cool soils and need a night temperature of 22C/72F for maximum yield. For a good crop they need 150 days of frost free weather, but using a sandy soil and raised bed you can heat the soil up quicker and get your sweet potatoes in the ground by late May. Covering the soil with black plastic will keep the soil warmer and so extend the growing season a bit.

When growing sweet potatoes, you start with young sweet potato plants which are referred to as slips. Sometimes they are called poles, transplants or draws and are tall sprouts grown from the previous crop, kind of like seed potatoes. A single sweet potato produces many slips.

Although you can start your own plants off, most people buy slips as usually they are 6 to 9 inches long with at least 5 leaves. If you buy certified plants, then you know they are disease free. Buying pre-grown slips is a great way for someone in a more northerly climate to get a head start on growing their sweet potatoes.

Sweet potatoes are tough and will survive mailing, but remove them from the packaging as soon as they arrive. Put the roots in water for 24 hours to give them a pick me up so they recover from their journey through the mail system. You can pack the roots with damp soil or peat moss and store them for about a week but it is better to get them into the ground as soon as you can.

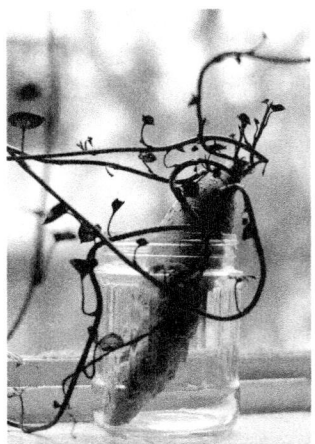

There are two types of sweet potato, one has moist flesh and the other has drier flesh. Most of the popular eating varieties are the moist fleshed varieties that are better at converting starch into sugar while cooking so they are sweeter in taste. The dry versions are not widely grown commercially.

Some of the more common varieties found are:

- Beauregard – this variety has a nice orange flesh with a reddish orange skin. It is a new variety and matures in around 90 days, producing a high yield.
- Bush Porto Rico – with a deep orange flesh covered with a copperish skin, this is a great variety for baking and requires less space. This variety matures in around 100 days.
- Centennial – this variety matures in 100 days, hence the name and has a soft, orange flesh with a fine grain. The roots are a tapered

shape and produce a high yield. Because of their yield and that they store very well makes it the most popular commercially grown variety in the USA.

- Georgia Jet – a very fast growing variety that is good for people further north as it matures in around 90 days. The skin is a lovely red color and the flesh is a deep orange.
- Jewell – maturing in 100 days this variety has a moist orange flesh covered with a copper colored skin. The vines grow vigorously produce good sized sweet potatoes that store very well.
- Vardaman – a golden yellow skin with a deep reddish orange flesh. Maturing in 100 days it is a bush variety that has unusual purple leaves.
- White Triumph – also known as White Yam this variety has a white skin with a dry white flesh. It matures in 100 days and is one of the oldest varieties of sweet potato growing on very compact vines.

As you can see most varieties of sweet potato take at least four months to grow and those months need to be frost free. The plants love hot weather and can be grown in a polytunnel in more northerly areas.

If you are starting your own slips, you need to sprout them about 8 weeks before you want to plant them. For anyone further north, buy 6 to 8 week slips as you can get a bit of a head start on avoiding the weather.

It is worth preparing the soil before you plant your sweet potatoes by digging in some fine compost or very well-rotted manure. The potatoes also appreciate some 5-10-10 fertilizer being dug in at a rate of about 3 pounds of fertilizer for each 100 feet of planting row. For a sandy soil increase this to 5 pounds.

Before planting, dig the soil over to about 10 inches. Sweet potatoes benefit from being planted in a raised bed containing a sandy soil as the soil warms quicker.

Plant sweet potato slips about 30-45cm/12-18" between plants in ridges. The rows need to be between 90-120cm/36-48" apart, depending on the size of the variety you are growing.

Put the slips in the ground so that the first leaves are under the soil. Firm down the soil and make a shallow depression around your planting area. This helps the water get directly to the roots where it is most needed. Water them in with a high phosphorous fertilizer and then water frequently for the first week or so as they settle in.

Keep the weeds down as sweet potatoes aren't too keen on competition. About a month after planting, mulch the area around the plants which helps to keep the weeds down as well as help the soil retain moisture. They benefit from another 3 pounds of 5-10-10 fertilizer being dug in per 100 feet.

During hot weather, give your sweet potatoes a really deep watering otherwise the plants dry out and do not mature fully.

Harvesting is typically from late September to mid-October, though for more northern areas dig them up just before a frost. Dig the roots out carefully as the potatoes bruise very easily. Once harvested, put them somewhere warm and humid to cure before storing.

Sweet potatoes are good fun to grow though you may struggle if you are too far north. So long as you get a decent amount of frost free time then these can be grown. They are an unusual crop to grow and are worth growing if you can.

Delicious Potato Recipes

Potatoes are a staple part of the Western diet and are a very versatile vegetable. There are so many different dishes you can cook with it that recipes would take up a book by themselves! I have included some of my favorite and most interesting recipes for you to enjoy.

One thing I will say though is you really ought to invest in an air fryer to cook your potatoes in. This is by far the best way I have found to make fries (chips), roast potatoes, tatter totts and many other fried potato dishes. It is very healthy as it uses little fat, you just parboil the potatoes before you put them in the air fryer. The potatoes crisp up nicely and str fluffy on the inside. Since buying one, it has become an essential kitchen gadget and I wouldn't want to be without it!

Garlic Rosemary Roasted Potatoes
I love this dish, though miss out the garlic if you don't like it. Sage is another herb that works well with rosemary or by itself too. These are absolutely delicious and the herbs really add flavor to the potatoes. It takes about 45 minutes to make and serves 6 people.

Ingredients:
- 900g/2lb russet potatoes (peeled and cut into ¾" chunks)
- 2 garlic cloves (minced)
- 1 tablespoon fresh rosemary (chopped)
- 1 tablespoon extra-virgin olive oil
- ½ teaspoon salt
- ¼ teaspoon freshly ground black pepper

Method:
1. Preheat your oven to 230C/450F and put a rack in the upper third of the oven
2. Parboil the potatoes for between 5 to 10 minutes until you can score them easily with a knife
3. Drain the potatoes and toss them in a bowl with the garlic, rosemary, oil, salt and pepper
4. Roast the potatoes in a roasting tin, turning every 10 to 15 minutes for 30 to 35 minutes until golden brown on the outside and tender on the inside

Golden Potato Gnocchi

A surprisingly tasty dish that is fun to make. It serves 4 people and takes about 2 hours 45 minutes to make.

Ingredients:
- 5 medium sized Russet potatoes (washed and peeled)
- 4 fried or poached eggs
- 3 garlic cloves (sliced thinly)
- 2 eggs (beaten)
- 1 shallot (minced)
- 2 cups all-purpose (plain) flour
- 1 to 2 cups of steamed, grilled or roasted vegetables, e.g. mushrooms, peppers, etc.
- 6 tablespoons unsalted butter
- 4 tablespoons seasonal pesto (e.g. arugula)
- 1 teaspoon salt

Method:
1. Boil the potatoes for about 35 to 40 minutes until they are tender
2. Mill the potatoes in a food mill and then mix in the egg, flour and salt
3. Knead for 4 or 5 minutes until it becomes dry to the touch; you may need to add a little bit more flour if it is too sticky
4. Roll the mixture out into ropes about an inch thick
5. Chop these ropes into 1" sized chunks
6. In batches (3 to 4 typically) throw these into a pot of salted boil water for a couple of minutes until they float
7. When they float, remove them from the boiling water and immediately transfer to a bowl of iced water
8. Heat a tablespoon of the butter in a pan and then sauté the garlic and shallots for a few minutes until they become translucent

9. Remove them from the pan, drain and put to one side
10. Sauté the gnocchi in the same pan with the rest of the butter until they are a golden brown color
11. Stir in the rest of the ingredients, except the eggs, and cook through
12. Serve in bowls topped with a fried egg and seasoned to taste

Multi-Colored Kebabs

These are a great, colorful dish that takes about 50 minutes to prepare and cook, serving four people. It's very tasty and can be served with thick potato wedges or fries.

Sauce Ingredients:
- ½ cup tomato sauce
- ¼ cup brown sugar (don't pack this down)
- ¼ cup ketchup
- 1 tablespoon cider vinegar
- 1 teaspoon garlic powder

Kebab Ingredients:
- 570g/1¼lb raw chicken breast (boneless and skinless, cut into 1" cubes)
- 540g/1lb blue or purple potatoes (cut into 1" chunks)
- 1 large onion (cut into 1" chunks)
- 1 red bell pepper (cut into 1" chunks)
- 2 tablespoons extra-virgin olive oil
- ½ teaspoon smoked paprika
- ¼ teaspoon onion powder
- ¼ teaspoon garlic powder
- ¼ teaspoon salt
- ¼ teaspoon black pepper

Method:
1. If you are using wooden skewers (you need 8) then soak in water for 20 minutes first to prevent them from burning
2. Mix together all the sauce ingredients in a glass bowl until thoroughly combined
3. Put the potato chunks into a microwaveable bowl with two tablespoons of water. Cover and cook on full power for 2 minutes then stir and cook for another 2 minutes until slightly softened
4. Drain the liquid from the potatoes

5. Add the onion powder, garlic powder, paprika, oil and an eighth of a teaspoon each of black pepper and salt, tossing well to ensure the potatoes are well coated
6. Season the chicken with ¼ teaspoon each of salt and black pepper
7. Alternating, thread the bell pepper, potato, onion and chicken onto the skewers
8. Spray a grill with a non-stick spray and heat to a medium to high heat
9. Grill the kebabs for around 5 minutes ensuring the grill cover is down
10. Flip the kebabs and grill for between 6 and 8 minutes (grill cover down again) until the chicken is thoroughly cooked and the potato is soft
11. Serve with the sauce

Vegetable Mashed Potatoes
This is nice variation on the normal mashed potatoes that takes about 20 minutes to make. It produces enough for 4 people.

Ingredients:
- 570g/1¼lb Russet potatoes
- 1 small onion (chopped)
- ½ cup shredded zucchini (courgette)
- ½ cup zero fat plain yogurt
- ½ cup fat free milk
- ⅓ cup carrot (shredded)
- 1½ tablespoons low fat butter (or butter spread)
- ¼ teaspoon salt
- Freshly ground black pepper to taste

Method:
1. Put the potatoes (whole, don't poke holes in them) in a microwave safe dish and cover (if using plastic wrap poke a small hole in the wrap)
2. Microwave on high power for between 10 and 12 minutes, depending on the power of your microwave
3. While the potatoes are in the microwave, sauté the onions in the butter on a medium heat for about 10 minutes
4. Add the carrot and zucchini, cooking for a further 3 minutes
5. Remove the potatoes from the microwave and mash well
6. Stir in the zucchini and carrots, milk and yogurt then season to taste

7. Heat for another couple of minutes if necessary and serve

Loaded Baked Potato

This is a great, quick meal to make as you prepare everything else while the potato is cooking. Remember to adjust the cooking time in the microwave depending on the size of the potato. You can also crisp it up nicely by putting it in a hot oven for a few minutes after microwaving it.

Ingredients:
- A baking potato (whatever size you like)
- 1 cup baby spinach
- ½ cup cottage cheese (flavored or low fat – it's up to you)
- ¼ cup marinara sauce
- 1 tablespoon mozzarella cheese (or cheddar)
- Italian herbs mixture (fresh or dried)

Method:
1. Pierce the potato with a fork a few times and microwave for between 4 and 10 minutes (turning at least once) depending on its size
2. In a bowl mix together the baby spinach with the marinara sauce and cottage cheese
3. Once the potato is cooked through, slice it open and stuff with this cottage cheese mixture
4. Sprinkle with the cheese and herbs
5. Microwave for 1 minute more to heat throughout

Baked Barbecue Fries

I love fries of any sort and these are particularly nice because of the spices and barbecue sauce. Use your favorite sauce here, there are plenty to choose from or use your home made sauce. It's up to you! This recipe will make enough for 4 people and take about half an hour to make.

Ingredients:
- 680g/1½lb Russet potatoes (scrubbed)
- ¼ cup barbecue sauce
- 1 tablespoon olive oil
- 1 teaspoon onion powder
- 1 teaspoon garlic powder
- ½ teaspoon coarsely ground black pepper
- ½ teaspoon sea salt

- Sprigs of fresh rosemary
- Salt
- Freshly ground black pepper
- Olive oil cooking spray

Method:
- Preheat your oven to 220C/425F and spray a large baking tray with the olive oil cooking spray
- Microwave the potatoes (covered – remember to poke holes in any plastic wrap) for between 3 and 4 minutes, depending on the strength of the microwave and size of the potatoes
- Allow the potatoes to cool before cutting into wedges or fries
- Place the potatoes into a large bowl and toss well with the olive oil
- Spread the potatoes out on your baking tray in a single layer
- In a separate bowl, mix together the spices until well combined
- Brush the potatoes with the barbecue sauce, then sprinkle with seasoning
- Bake for about 10 minutes
- Spray the potatoes with olive oil, turn and spray again before baking for another 10 minutes then spraying again
- Mash together the rosemary, salt and pepper (use the back of a spoon) and sprinkle over the cooked potatoes, tossing well to ensure thoroughly coated
- Bake for a further 5 minutes to heat through and serve

Thanksgiving Mashed Potatoes
This is a classic recipe for a traditional thanksgiving. Of course, it can be used with your Sunday roast or with any meal, but definitely worth a try. This recipe makes enough for 8 servings and takes approximately 40 minutes to cook.

Ingredients:
- 900g/2lb russet potatoes (about 4 large ones)
- ¾ cup milk
- 6 tablespoons unsalted butter
- 1 teaspoon salt
- Freshly ground black pepper to taste

Method:
1. Peel the potatoes then rinse in cold water
2. Cut into quarters, place in a pan
3. Cover with cold water and partially cover the pot
4. Bring to the boil then uncover and add a teaspoon of salt
5. Reduce the heat to a gentle boil
6. After 10 to 12 minutes the potatoes should be tender when you pierce them with a fork
7. Drain the potatoes and return to the warm pan (on a low heat) for a minute or two to evaporate off any excess water
8. Meanwhile, heat the milk and butter in a smaller saucepan together until the butter is melted but do not boil
9. Remove the potatoes from the heat and mash (or use a ricer/food mill)
10. Stir in the milk mixture, a little at a time, until you get your preferred consistency
11. Season to taste and serve immediately

Shrimp and Potato Croquettes
An interesting variation on the potato croquette that is rather pleasant. This recipe makes about 20 and takes about 40 minutes to make.

Ingredients:
- 450g/1lb medium shrimp (peeled and deveined)
- 2 garlic cloves (minced)
- 2 large eggs (beaten)
- 1 shallot (minced)
- 2½ cups panko breadcrumbs
- 2 cups mashed potato
- ⅓ cup Cheddar or Monterey Jack cheese (shredded)
- ¼ cup mayonnaise
- 2 tablespoons Sriracha (to taste)
- 1 tablespoon olive oil (plus extra for frying)
- ¼ teaspoon salt
- ⅛ teaspoon freshly ground black pepper

Method:
1. Put the olive oil in a skillet and heat on a medium heat
2. Add the shallot, garlic and shrimp and season to taste
3. Cook for about three minutes, stirring often, until the shrimp is pink and cooked through

4. Put this mixture into your food processor and pulse until it is finely chopped
5. Now add the cheese and mashed potato, pulsing until it is mixed together
6. Put the eggs and breadcrumbs into separate bowls
7. Use a small ice cream scoop (around 2 tablespoons) to scoop out balls of the shrimp and potato mixture
8. Work in batches of 6, shape each ball into an egg shape
9. Put each ball of shrimp mixture onto a spoon and dip into the egg, ensuring it is coated all over
10. Then dip into the breadcrumbs, again ensuring it is well covered
11. Repeat this process until you have used all of the shrimp and potato mixture
12. Pour the olive oil into a non-stick skillet until it is about an inch deep
13. Heat this on a medium heat until hot enough for frying – test by dropping a few breadcrumbs into the oil
14. Cooking in batches of 6, brown the croquettes on all sides, putting the cooked croquettes on paper towels to drain excess oil
15. Continue until all the croquettes are cooked
16. The sauce is made by mixing the Sriracha with the mayonnaise
17. Serve the croquettes hot with the sauce on the side

Rainbow Potato Salad

This is a really colorful dish that is great to serve. Most people don't realize there are such a variety of potatoes so it is an eye opening for them. Try adding some golden beetroot to make this more interesting. This dish produces enough for 8 servings and takes about an hour to make.

Ingredients:
- 2 red potatoes (cut into 1" pieces)
- 2 purple potatoes (cut into 1" pieces)
- 2 cups fresh green beans (trimmed and halved)
- 1 cup zucchini/courgette (halved and sliced)
- 1 cup fresh corn kernels
- 1 cup yellow squash (halved and sliced)
- 1 cup grape tomatoes (halved)
- ¼ cup shallots (sliced)
- ¼ cup fresh lemon juice
- 4 tablespoons olive oil (divided)
- ½ tablespoon fresh thyme (chopped)

- 2 teaspoons sugar
- ½ teaspoon pepper (divided)
- ½ teaspoon salt (divided)

Method:
1. Preheat your oven to 200C/400F
2. Toss the potatoes in a large bowl with a tablespoon of olive oil
3. Sprinkle with ¼ teaspoon each of salt and pepper
4. Roast for about 30 minutes, turning once until browned and tender
5. Put to one side and allow to cool
6. Put the green beans into a large pan on a medium heat together with 3 tablespoons of water
7. Cook for 2 to 3 minutes until the beans turn a bright green color and the water has evaporated
8. Add a tablespoon of olive oil together with the corn, zucchini and yellow squash
9. Cook for around 6 or 7 minutes until the vegetables are tender and crisp
10. Add the time and the rest of the salt and pepper
11. Cook for a couple more minutes until fragrant
12. Remove from the heat and add the grape tomatoes and leave to cool
13. Once both mixtures are at room temperature, add the potatoes to the vegetables
14. In a small bowl mix together the sugar and lemon juice
15. While whisking, drizzle in 2 tablespoons of oil
16. Add the shallots and stir well
17. Drizzle this vinaigrette over the potato mixture and carefully toss so everything is well coated
18. Season to taste and serve chilled or at room temperature

Slim Fries

This is a great variation on normal fries that are well worth a try. Again, these work very well in an air fryer. This dish will take about 40 minutes to make and produce enough for 6 servings.

Ingredients:
- 680g/1½ lbs potatoes of a similar size (cut lengthwise into ½" thick slices
- 1 garlic clove (minced)
- 3 tablespoons olive oil
- 2 teaspoons fresh rosemary (finely chopped)

- ½ teaspoon salt

Method:
1. Preheat a grill pan on a medium heat
2. Mix all the ingredients together in a large bowl, until thoroughly combined
3. Grill in a single layer until browned on the bottom
4. Turn and grill for a further 10 minutes until cooked through and brown all over

Star Mash Chips
These are an unusual type of chip and are really tasty. They are great to serve to children and guests, being quite unusual to look at. This makes between 45 and 50 chips and takes about 35 minutes to make.

Ingredients:
- 3 cups mashed potato (leftovers can be used – needs to be warmed)
- 57g/2oz goat cheese (crumbled)
- 1 egg (lightly beaten)
- 2 teaspoons fresh thyme (minced)
- 2 teaspoons fresh chives (thinly sliced)
- 1 teaspoon fresh rosemary (minced)
- Salt and pepper to taste

Method:
1. Beat the mash, egg and cheese together in a large bowl until well combined
2. Gently fold in the herbs before seasoning to taste
3. Put a star tip on your piping bag and fill it with the potato mixture
4. Pipe small stars onto a greased baking sheet
5. Season with cracked black pepper and salt
6. Cook in a preheated (190C/375F) oven for between 18 and 22 minutes until golden brown
7. Remove from the oven and cool for 5 minutes before eating

Spicy Stuffed Potatoes
This is a great dish to make and has a nice tang to it. Well worth a go.

Potato Ingredients:
- 12 potatoes about 2" across
- ½ cup cheddar cheese (shredded)
- 2 tablespoons olive oil
- 2 teaspoons red jalapeno pepper (finely chopped)
- 1 teaspoon garlic powder
- Salt and pepper to taste
- Fresh chopped cilantro (coriander) to garnish

Guacamole Ingredients:
- 1 avocado
- 2 teaspoons fresh chives (finely chopped)
- ½ lime (juiced)
- Salt and pepper to taste

Method:
1. Preheat your oven to 200C/400F
2. Trim a little off one side of each of the potatoes so they will lie flat
3. Put the potatoes into a large bowl and drizzle over the olive oil
4. Add the garlic powder and season to taste
5. Toss well until evenly coated
6. Lay the potatoes on a baking sheet lined with parchment paper
7. Cook for between 30 and 35 minutes until the potatoes are tender
8. Leave the potatoes to cool until you can handle them
9. Cut ¼" from the top of each potato
10. Using a very small spoon scoop out the middle of each potato
11. Put the hollowed out potatoes back on the baking sheet facing upwards
12. Divide the cheese between each potato, stuffing the hollow
13. Season to taste and then bake for about 5 minutes until the cheese just starts to melt
14. Meanwhile, pit and peel the avocado
15. Dice the avocado and put in a medium sized bowl
16. Add the lime juice, chives and season to taste, mashing it all together until you get a chunky paste
17. Allow the potatoes to cool slightly before topping with the guacamole
18. Garnish with jalapeno pepper and cilantro before serving

Potato and Spinach Baja

This is a great Indian dish to make with a nice spiced taste. It takes about 30 minutes to make and produces enough to serve four people.

Ingredients:

- 3 large potatoes (russet if possible cut into ½" strips)
- 4 green Thai bird chillies (de-seeded and thinly sliced)
- 3 garlic cloves (minced)
- 1 large red onion (thinly sliced)
- 1 bunch fresh spinach (cut into strips)
- 2 tablespoon curry powder
- 1 tablespoon ground cumin
- 1 tablespoon turmeric
- Olive oil
- Salt

Method:

1. Boil the potatoes until soft
2. Oil a non-stick skillet with olive oil
3. Cook the onion, stirring often, until browned
4. Add the chillies, garlic, cumin, turmeric and curry powder, and season with salt
5. Cook until brown and fragrant
6. In another non-stick skillet, heat 2 tablespoons of olive oil
7. Cook the spinach until it becomes dry and crispy
8. Remove the spinach from the pan
9. In the same skillet, heat another 2 tablespoons of oil
10. Cook the potatoes until browned
11. Add the onions and spinach, cooking until crisp and brown all over

TIPS FOR GROWING THE BEST POTATOES

Growing potatoes is great fun and I'd like to share with you some of my best tips to ensure you get a good crop of healthy, delicious potatoes.

- Drainage – this is vital for your potatoes as they hate being waterlogged. If growing in a clay soil, dig in gravel beneath them to act as a water soak. Stand containers on bricks to stop them getting waterlogged.
- Remember to earth up your potatoes, or at least protect them from the light. This stops the potatoes turning green and ensures good growth. If you see any potatoes peeking up above the ground, cover them with a couple of inches of soil.
- Potatoes love the sun, so ensure your potato bed is not in the shade. Move containers to ensure they get plenty of sun during the day.
- Potatoes are very hungry plants and appreciate regular feeding during the growing season. Nettle or comfrey tea make for a good feed as does any good quality plant food. It is best to water them in the morning so the leaves have time to dry out fully during the day. Wet leaves overnight can encourage fungal growth and diseases.
- Always water at the base of the plant as damp leaves encourage blight and other fungal infections. Aim to get the water on the soil, directly to the roots.
- Potatoes are thirsty plants too and need plenty of water to produce good sized potatoes. Collect water, if you can, on your plot as you will go through a lot. Make sure you water regularly and deeply so the water goes down to the roots and tubers where it is needed.
- Pinching out the flowers helps your plant produce larger potatoes. The flowers turn into seeds and the potatoes will put their energy

into those rather than the tubers if the flowers are left in place.

- Check your plants regularly for signs of blight and, if you are prone to blight ,then start to spray before blight rears its ugly head.
- Check your plants often for signs of pests or other diseases. If you can catch them early, then you can start to treat them before they spread to the rest of your crop.
- Be aware that slugs love potatoes and small slugs that live in the soil can cause a lot of damage. If your vegetable plot has a lot of slugs on, then using slug pellets or another deterrent may help preserve your crop and reduce damage. Just be careful that you do not harm wildlife that eats slugs such as frogs and birds.
- Dig up your potatoes when the weather is dry and leave them for an hour or two in a single layer to dry before moving them to storage.
- Handle your potatoes with care as they easily bruise which will affect their ability to be stored.
- Any potatoes that are damaged should not be stored and are best used over the next few days.
- When digging up your potatoes, start a reasonable distance from the plant to try and avoid damaging any of your crop.
- Use a fork to dig up your potatoes as it is easier to lift them. If you do damage any, then they are just speared rather than cut into pieces by a spade.
- Grow first early potatoes and get them into the ground on time if your area suffers from blight – you will miss the blight and still get a good crop.
- Keep the weeds down around your potatoes as this helps prevent the spread of disease and removes a potential habitat for pests. It also stops the potatoes having to compete with the faster growing weeds for resources.

Endnote

Growing potatoes is really good fun and very easy to do. They are one of the most popular crops to grow at home and everyone loves digging through the soil and finding a potato in the ground. It is one of the must have experiences of growing your own.

Freshly harvested potatoes taste fantastic and by growing a number of varieties you can grow potatoes that are good for mashing, chipping, baking and so on. You can also grow some of the more unusual varieties that you won't find in the stores. With over 5000 different varieties, there are plenty to choose from but you will find some of the varieties not found in stores are the best. Personally, I love pink fir apple and Nicola potatoes but have yet to see any of these in a shop.

Potatoes are best started from certified seed potatoes because you know you are starting off with potatoes that do not have any diseases. Although you can grow potatoes from store bought potatoes successfully, you do not have any assurances that these are disease free and you could end up introducing infection into your vegetable plot.

Potatoes are low maintenance plants with the tender new growth being susceptible to frost damage. The main challenge with growing potatoes is preventing damage to the tubers through wire worms and slugs. If the soil is particularly damp or there is a lot of rain, then you can find your potatoes rot in the ground so lift them quickly if that is the case in your area. And yes, I have been known to dig potatoes during heavy rain.

As potatoes are easily infected by blight, you need to be much more diligent in your crop rotation with potatoes than you would with some other plants. If blight is in the soil, then you can find your crop destroyed before it has had the chance to mature so never grow your potatoes in the same patch of soil two years running. Ideally, you want to leave 3 or 4 years before growing in the same area again. Some gardeners I know grow in the same spot every year and any time there is a sign of problems, they spray the soil with a diluted solution of Jeyes fluid. As I am not yet entirely sure of the effect this has on the micro-organisms that live in the soil, I haven't tried it, but these people have been doing it for years and produce a good crop every year.

Container growing works really well with potatoes, though you need to be careful not to plant too many tubers in any container. Too many in a single container results in a smaller crop rather than a larger one. You also need to be much more diligent in feeding and watering too because they are entirely dependent on you for that.

Potatoes are one of my favorite crops to grow and every year I try to grow plenty. My personal choice is to grow them in containers rather than the soil because it is much easier to harvest them from containers, but it is your choice where you grow yours. They are a rewarding crop to grow and you can store maincrop potatoes for up to six months in ideal conditions.

With a combination of first early, second early, maincrop and late varieties you can have an almost continual supply though the year. Stored properly you will find you even have potatoes during the colder months and spring.

For anyone who is wondering about growing potatoes I would say go for it. They are a fantastic crop to grow and really good fun. Kids love them and even adults get a twinge of pleasure from rooting around in the soil and finding potatoes hiding in the ground.

Enjoy growing your potatoes and please remember to leave a review if you have enjoyed this book.

ABOUT JASON

Jason has been a keen gardener for over twenty years, having taken on numerous weed infested patches and turned them into productive vegetable gardens.

One of his first gardening experiences was digging over a 400 square foot garden in its entirety and turning it into a vegetable garden, much to the delight of his neighbors who all got free vegetables! It was through this experience that he discovered his love of gardening and started to learn more and more about the subject.

His first encounter with a greenhouse resulted in a tomato infested greenhouse but he soon learnt how to make the most of a greenhouse and now grows a wide variety of plants from grapes to squashes to tomatoes and more. Of course, his wife is delighted with his greenhouse as it means the windowsills in the house are no longer filled with seed trays every spring.

He is passionate about helping people learn to grow their own fresh produce and enjoy the many benefits that come with it, from the exercise of gardening to the nutrition of freshly picked produce. He often says that when you've tasted a freshly picked tomato you'll never want to buy another one from a store again!

Jason is also very active in the personal development community, having written books on self-help, including subjects such as motivation and confidence. He has also recorded over 80 hypnosis programs, being a fully qualified clinical hypnotist which he sells from his website www.MusicForChange.com.

He hopes that this book has been a pleasure for you to read and that you have learned a lot about the subject and welcomes your feedback either directly or through an Amazon review. This feedback is used to improve his books and provide better quality information for his readers.

Jason also loves to grow giant and unusual vegetables and is still planning on breaking the 400lb barrier with a giant pumpkin. He hopes that with his new allotment plot he'll be able to grow even more exciting vegetables to share with his readers.

OTHER GARDENING BOOKS BY JASON

Please check out my other gardening books on Amazon, available in Kindle and paperback.

A Gardener's Guide to Weeds - How To Use Common Garden Weeds For Food, Health, Beauty And More

Ever wondered about the weeds that take over your garden? You may be surprised to know that these weeds are the ancestors of many of the crops we regularly eat and used to be the staple diet for humans. This book teaches you all about weeds including how to use them in your garden and kitchen and their traditional medicinal uses as well as the folklore and myths associated with them. A fascinating insight into the gardener's foe!

An Allotment Journal – Plan Your Fruit and Vegetable Garden

Learn how to plan your vegetable garden or allotment for success as you discover the techniques for growing a bountiful harvest. Discover how to track what you are growing, where you are growing it and how to make the most of your space. Learn techniques such as crop rotation and succession planting to make the most of your space together with monthly jobs at the allotment, a seed planting schedule plus growing guides for over 50 different vegetables.

An Introduction To Smallholdings – Getting Started On Your Smallholding

Thinking about getting a smallholding? Find out everything you need to consider from the best location to what equipment you need. Talking about everything relating to a smallholding such as how to make an income, what to grow and sell, keeping animals and more, this guide will walk you through everything you must know before living the smallholding dream.

.

Berry Gardening – The Complete Guide to Berry Gardening from Gooseberries to Boysenberries and More

Who doesn't love fresh berries? Find out how you can grow many of the popular berries at home such as marionberries and blackberries and some of the more unusual like honeyberries and goji berries. A step by step guide to growing your own berries including pruning, propagating and more. Discover how you can grow a wide variety of berries at home in your garden or on your balcony.

Canning and Preserving at Home – A Complete Guide to Canning, Preserving and Storing Your Produce

A complete guide to storing your home-grown fruits and vegetables. Learn everything from how to freeze your produce to canning, making jams, jellies, and chutneys to dehydrating and more. Everything you need to know about storing your fresh produce, including some unusual methods of storage, some of which will encourage children to eat fresh fruit!

Companion Planting Secrets – Organic Gardening to Deter Pests and Increase Yield

Learn the secrets of natural and organic pest control with companion planting. This is a great way to increase your yield, produce better quality plants and work in harmony with nature. By attracting beneficial insects to your garden, you can naturally keep down harmful pests and reduce the damage they cause. You probably grow many of these companion plants already, but by repositioning them, you can reap the many benefits of this natural method of gardening.

Container Gardening - Growing Vegetables, Herbs & Flowers in Containers

A step by step guide showing you how to create your very own container garden. Whether you have no garden, little space or you want to grow specific plants, this book guides you through everything you need to know about planting a container garden from the different types of pots, to which plants thrive in containers to handy tips helping you avoid the common mistakes people make with containers..

Cooking With Zucchini - Delicious Recipes, Preserves and More With Courgettes: How To Deal With A Glut Of Zucchini And Love It!

Getting too many zucchinis from your plants? This book teaches you how to grow your own courgettes at home as well as showing you the many different varieties you could grow. Packed full of delicious recipes, you will learn everything from the famous zucchini chocolate cake to delicious main courses, snacks, and Paleo diet friendly raw recipes. The must have guide for anyone dealing with a glut of zucchini.

Environmentally Friendly Gardening - - Your Guide to a Sustainable Eco-Friendly Garden

A guide to making your garden more environmentally friendly, from looking after beneficial insects and wildlife, to saving water and reducing plastic use. There is a lot you can do to reduce your reliance on chemicals and work in harmony with nature, while still having a beautiful and productive garden. This book details many things you can easily do to become more eco-friendly in your garden.

Greenhouse Gardening - A Beginners Guide to Growing Fruit and Vegetables All Year Round

A complete, step by step guide to owning a greenhouse. Learn everything you need to know from sourcing greenhouses to building foundations to ensuring it survives high winds. This handy guide will teach you everything you need to know to grow a wide range of plants in your greenhouse, including tomatoes, chilies, squashes, zucchini and much more.

Growing Brassicas – Growing Cruciferous Vegetables from Broccoli to Mooli to Wasabi and More

Brassicas are renowned for their health benefits and are packed full of vitamins. They are easy to grow at home, but beset by problems. Find out how you can grow these amazing vegetables at home, including the incredibly beneficial plants broccoli and maca. Includes step by step growing guides plus delicious recipes for every recipe!

Growing Chillies – A Beginners Guide to Growing, Using & Surviving Chillies

Ever wanted to grow super-hot chillies? Or maybe you just want to grow your own chillies to add some flavor to your food? This book is your complete, step-by-step guide to growing chillies at home. With topics from selecting varieties to how to germinate seeds, you will learn everything you need to know to grow chillies successfully, even the notoriously difficult to grow varieties such as Carolina Reaper. With recipes for sauces, meals and making your own chilli powder, you'll find everything you need to know to grow your own chilli plants.

Growing Fruit: The Complete Guide to Growing Fruit at Home

This is a complete guide to growing fruit from apricots to walnuts and everything in between. You will learn how to choose fruit plants, how to grow and care for them, how to store and preserve the fruit and much more. With recipes, advice, and tips this is the perfect book for anyone who wants to learn more about growing fruit at home, whether beginner or experienced gardener.

.

Growing Garlic – A Complete Guide to Growing, Harvesting & Using Garlic

Everything you need to know to grow this popular plant. Whether you are growing normal garlic or elephant garlic for cooking or health, you will find this book contains all the information you need. Traditionally a difficult crop to grow with a long growing season, you'll learn the exact conditions garlic needs, how to avoid the common problems people encounter and how to store your garlic for use all year round. A complete, step-by-step guide showing you precisely how to grow garlic at home.

Growing Giant Pumpkins – How to Grow Massive Pumpkins At Home

A complete step-by-step guide detailing everything you need to know to produce pumpkins weighing hundreds of pounds, if not edging into the thousands! Anyone can grow giant pumpkins at home, and this book gives you the insider secrets of the giant pumpkin growers showing you how to avoid the mistakes people commonly make when trying to grow a giant pumpkin. This is a complete guide detailing everything from preparing the soil to getting the right seeds to germinating the seeds and caring for your pumpkins.

Growing Herbs – A Beginners Guide To Growing, Using, Harvesting and Storing Herbs

A comprehensive guide to growing herbs at home, detailing 49 different herbs. Learn everything you need to know to grow these herbs from their preferred soil conditions to how to harvest and propagate them and more. Including recipes for health and beauty plus delicious dishes to make in your kitchen. This step-by-step guide is designed to teach you all about growing herbs at home, from a few herbs in containers to a fully-fledged herb garden.

Growing Lavender: Growing, Using, Cooking and Healing with Lavender

A complete guide to growing and using this beautiful plant. Find out about the hundreds of different varieties of lavender and how you can grow this bee friendly plant at home. With hundreds of uses in crafts, cooking and healing, this plant has a long history of association with humans. Discover today how you can grow lavender at home and enjoy this amazing herb.

Growing Tomatoes: Your Guide to Growing Delicious Tomatoes

This is the definitive guide to growing delicious and fresh tomatoes at home. Teaching you everything from selecting seeds to planting and caring for your tomatoes as well as diagnosing problems this is the ideal book for anyone who wants to grow their own tomatoes. You will learn the secrets of a successful tomato grower and learn about the many different types of tomato you could grow, most of which are not available in any shops! A comprehensive must have guide..

How to Compost – Turn Your Waste into Brown Gold

This is a complete step by step guide to making your own compost at home. Vital to any gardener, this book will explain everything from setting up your compost heap to how to ensure you get fresh compost in just a few weeks. You will learn the techniques for producing highly nutritious compost that will help your plants grow while recycling your kitchen waste. A must have handbook for any gardener who wants their plants to benefit from home-made compost.

How to Grow Potatoes - The Guide To Choosing, Planting and Growing in Containers Or the Ground

Learn everything you need to know about growing potatoes at home. Discover the wide variety of potatoes you can grow, many delicious varieties you will never see in the shops. Find out the best way to grow potatoes at home, how to protect your plants from the many pests and diseases and how to store your harvest so you can enjoy fresh potatoes over winter. A complete step by step guide telling you everything you need to know to grow potatoes at home successfully.

Hydroponics: A Beginners Guide to Growing Food without Soil

Hydroponics is growing plants without soil, which is a fantastic idea for indoor gardens. It is surprisingly easy to set up, once you know what you are doing and is significantly more productive and quicker than growing in soil. It doesn't even have to be expensive to get started, and the possibilities are endless. This book will tell you everything you need to know to get started growing flowers, vegetables and fruit hydroponically at home.

Indoor Gardening for Beginners: The Complete Guide to Growing Herbs, Flowers, Vegetables and Fruits in Your House

Discover how you can grow a wide variety of plants in your home. Whether you want to grow herbs for cooking, vegetables or a decorative plant display, this book tells you everything you need to know. Learn which plants to keep in your home to purify the air and remove harmful chemicals and how to successfully grow plants from cacti to flowers to carnivorous plants.

Keeping Chickens for Beginners – Keeping Backyard Chickens from Coops to Feeding to Care and More

Chickens are becoming very popular to keep at home, but it isn't something you should leap into without the right information. This book guides you through everything you need to know to keep chickens from decided what breed to what coop to how to feed them, look after them and keep your chickens healthy and producing eggs. This is your complete guide to owning chickens, with absolutely everything you need to know to get started and successfully keep chickens at home.

Raised Bed Gardening – A Guide to Growing Vegetables In Raised Beds

Learn why raised beds are such an efficient and effortless way to garden as you discover the benefits of no-dig gardening, denser planting and less bending, ideal for anyone who hates weeding or suffers from back pain. Easy to build and lasting for years I cannot recommend this method of gardening enough for its many benefits! You will learn everything you need to know to build your own raised beds, plant them and ensure they are highly productive.

Save Our Bees – Your Guide to Creating a Bee Friendly Environment

Find out how you can help save the bees and protect this insect that is vital to your food production and environment. Our modern lives have disrupted the bees to a point where many are dying off. Learn what you can do to help the bees no matter how much space you have at home! Discover what bees need, how you can provide it and all about the different types of bees! These misunderstood creatures are pretty much harmless and are fascinating insects.

Square Foot Gardening – Growing More in Less Space

Learn about this unique gardening style which enables you to grow more in less space. This dense planting method using nutrient rich soil to produce fantastic yields. You will learn exactly how to create your own square foot garden, how to create the perfect soil mix and exactly how to space your plants for maximum yields. You will find out what you can grow in a square foot garden as well as what to avoid growing plus helpful advice so you can make the most of your growing area. An in-depth guide to getting you started with your first square foot garden.

The Complete Allotment Guide - Volume 1 – Starting Out, Growing and Techniques: Everything You Need To Know To Grow Fruits and Vegetables

A complete guide to owning and allotment and growing fruits, vegetables and more. Find out the process of getting an allotment, what allotments are like and how they work. This guide is essential for anyone who has an allotment or is thinking about getting one, plus it will help any vegetable gardener grow more successfully.

Vertical Gardening: Maximum Productivity, Minimum Space

This is an exciting form of gardening allows you to grow large amounts of fruit and vegetables in small areas, maximizing your use of space. Whether you have a large garden, an allotment or just a small balcony, you will be able to grow more delicious fresh produce. Becoming more popular not just amongst gardeners but even with city planners, this is a fantastic gardening technique that significantly boosts your yield. Find out how I grew over 70 strawberry plants in just three feet of ground space and more in this detailed guide.

Worm Farming – Creating Compost at Home with Vermiculture

An in-depth guide to one of the hottest topics on the market as you learn how you can use worms to turn your kitchen scraps into a high quality, highly nutritious compost that will help your plants to thrive! Easy to set up, low cost and able to be done in a small corner of a shed or garage this is a fantastic way for anyone to make their own compost or even scale it up to create a highly profitable business. Discover how you can make one of the best composts on the market with kitchen waste and worms!

WANT MORE INSPIRING GARDENING IDEAS?

This book is part of the Inspiring Gardening Ideas series. Bringing you the best books anywhere on how to get the most from your garden or allotment. Please remember to leave a review on Amazon once you have finished this book as it helps me continually improve my books.

You can find out about more wonderful books just like this one at: www.GardeningWithJason.com

Follow me at www.YouTube.com/OwningAnAllotment for my video diary and tips. Join me on Facebook for regular updates and discussions at www.Facebook.com/OwningAnAllotment.

Find me on Instagram and Twitter as @allotmentowner where I post regular updates, offers and gardening news. Follow me today and let's catch up in person!

FREE BOOK!

Visit http://gardeningwithjason.com/your-free-book/ now for your free copy of my book "Environmentally Friendly Gardening" sent to your inbox. Discover today how you can become a more eco-friendly gardener and help us all make the world a better place.

This book is full of tips and advice, helping you to reduce your need for chemicals and work in harmony with nature to improve the environment. With the looming crisis, there is something we can all do in our gardens, no matter how big or small they are and they can still look fantastic!

Thank you for reading!

Printed in Great Britain
by Amazon

27094973R00056